$1.50
6/8

D0221781

Documents and Debates
The French Revolution

Documents and Debates

For the extended series, see the back cover of this book.

Documents and Debates
General Editor: John Wroughton, M.A., F.R.Hist.S.

The French Revolution

Leonard W. Cowie
M.A., Ph.D., F.R.Hist.S.

MACMILLAN

First published 1988 by
THE MACMILLAN PRESS LTD
Houndmills, Basingstoke, Hampshire RG21 2XS
and London
Companies and representatives
throughout the world

ISBN 0–333–43461–7

A catalogue record for this book is available
from the British Library.

Printed in China

Reprinted 1992, 1993

Contents

General Editor's Preface

This book forms part of a series entitled *Documents and Debates*, which is aimed primarily at sixth formers. The earlier volumes in the series each covered approximately one century of history, using material both from original documents and from modern historians. The more recent volumes, however, are designed in response to the changing trends in history examinations at 18 plus, most of which now demand the study of documentary sources and the testing of historical skills. Each volume therefore concentrates on a particular topic within a narrower span of time. It consists of eight sections, each dealing with a major theme in depth, illustrated by extracts drawn from primary sources. The series intends partly to provide experience for those pupils who are required to answer questions on documentary material at A-level, and partly to provide pupils of all abilities with a digestible and interesting collection of source material, which will extend the normal textbook approach.

This book is designed essentially for the pupil's own personal use. The author's introduction will put the period as a whole into perspective, highlighting the central issues, main controversies, available source material and recent developments. Although it is clearly not our intention to replace the traditional textbook, each section will carry its own brief introduction, which will set the documents into context. A wide variety of source material has been used in order to give the pupils the maximum amount of experience – letters, speeches, newspapers, memoirs, diaries, official papers, Acts of Parliament, Minute Books, accounts, local documents, family papers, etc. The questions vary in difficulty, but aim throughout to compel the pupil to think in depth by the use of unfamiliar material. Historical knowledge and understanding will be tested, as well as basic comprehension. Pupils will also be encouraged by the questions to assess the reliability of evidence, to recognise bias and emotional prejudice, to reconcile conflicting accounts and to extract the essential from the irrelevant. Some questions, *marked with an asterisk*, require knowledge outside the immediate extract and are intended for further research or discussion, based on the pupil's general knowledge of the period. Finally, we hope that students using this material will learn something of the nature of historical inquiry and the role of the historian.

John Wroughton

Acknowledgements

The author and publishers wish to thank the following who have kindly given permission for the use of copyright material.

Edward Arnold (Publishers) Ltd for extracts from *The French Revolution: the Fall of the Ancien Régime to the Thermidorian Reaction 1785–1795* by John Hardman, Documents of Modern History Series, 1981; Basil Blackwell Ltd for extracts from *French Revolution Documents 1787–92* ed. J. M. Roberts, 1966 and *English Witnesses of the French Revolution* by J. M. Thompson, 1938; Cambridge University Press for extracts from *Arthur Young: Travels in France during the Years 1787, 1788 and 1789* ed. C. Maxwell, 1950; The Folio Society for extracts from *Escape from Terror: The Journal of Madame de la Tour du Pin* translated, edited and with an introduction by Felice Harcourt, 1979; Libraire Armand Colin for extracts from *Les Ecrivains Politiques du XVIII Siècles* eds Albert Bayet and Françoise Albert, 1926.

Every effort has been made to trace all the copyright holders but if any have been inadvertently overlooked the publishers will be pleased to make the necessary arrangement at the first opportunity.

Introduction – What was the French Revolution?

British historians have produced a number of collections of extracts from contemporary documents about this subject, including H. Morse Stephens, *The Principal Speeches of the Statesmen and Orators of the French Revolution 1789–95* (2 vols, 1892), L. G. Wickham Legg, *Select Documents Illustrative of the History of the French Revolution* (2 vols, 1905), J. M. Thompson, *The French Revolution* (1933), J. M. Roberts, *French Revolution Documents 1787–92* (1966) and John Hardman, *French Revolution Documents 1792–5* (1973). The documents in these are in French, but those in John Hardman, *The French Revolution 1785–95* (1981), are in English, as also are those in more limited collections such as J. M. Thompson, *English Witnesses of the French Revolution* (1938), J. Gilchrist & W. J. Murray, *The Press in the French Revolution (1971)* and Michael Walzer, *Regicide and Revolution: Speeches at the Trial of Louis XVI* (1974). Use has been made for this book of such collections, translating the documents into English where necessary, and extracts have also been taken directly from a diversity of contemporary sources of French and other origin.

The eight chapters of this book attempt to reveal some of the main themes and issues raised by historians in considering the comprehensive question – What was the French Revolution? The extracts from documents indicate some of the evidence upon which discussion is based, and the questions upon the documents suggest the arguments and counter-arguments which have been advanced about 'the greatest of all revolutions' by writers in different countries:

I When did the French Revolution begin? Alfred Cobban, who was successively Reader and Professor of French History at University College, London, from 1937 to 1967, once gave an answer to this question which has become well known. He said that there were three things which everyone knew about this subject, but all of them were wrong. These were that the French Revolution happened in 1789, that it took place in Paris, and that it was a rising of the people. In fact, he said that it began as a breakdown of authority of the government; that it occurred in 1787 in the provinces; and that it was led by the nobility.

All historians have by no means been ready to accept this

substitution of one time scale for another; but there has recently been much interest taken in the causes of the French Revolution or rather, perhaps more realistically, in its 'origins' as suggested by William Doyle, *The Origins of the French Revolution* (1981). In this book, therefore, the first chapter gives a considerable amount of space to this subject, drawing the material mainly from those first years of the reign of Louis XVI (b. 1754, s. 1774, d. 1793), when the sovereign authority of the French crown, though outwardly unchanged, was nevertheless meeting mounting criticism as the country faced a number of worsening fiscal, economic, administrative and social crises. These, together with the failure to adopt the several political and legal reforms which were put forward during these years, form the major themes of this section.

II Some historians, including John M. Roberts, *The French Revolution* (1978), see the year 1785 as the beginning of something they call the pre-Revolution, and the second chapter of this book deals with this idea. Central to the national problems of this period were the inadequate resources of the royal treasury, and from it followed the political developments leading to the preliminary events which were to bring about the Revolution.

III This chapter opens with the meeting of the Estates-General on 5 May 1789, a date which many still recognise as the beginning of the Revolution. Outwardly it was no more than the assembly of an important, historic institution of the *ancien régime*, but in fact it marked the capitulation of the absolute monarchy. The financial situation had enabled the nobility to follow its traditional policy of seeking to exploit the crown's weakness to its own advantage. But this action enabled the third estate to assert its wishes, and this chapter shows it taking over the revolt for its own purposes, not foreseeing the intervention by the people which was soon to transform the situation.

IV The development and consequences of this violent extension of the Revolution is the theme of this chapter. The rising in Paris and the disturbances in the countryside are a reminder that there were many revolutions within the Revolution. The demands of the peasants were different from those of the urban insurgents. The peasants were eventually satisfied with the suppression of all feudal rights. Henceforward they stood aside from the Revolution, except in such districts as Brittany and La Vendée, where they rose in opposition to it. The Paris mob, however, continued to assert itself as a powerful force in the events of the Revolution.

V For the first eighteen months of the period of this chapter, the Assembly largely devoted itself to the work of reconstructing the kingdom, which had been interrupted by the disturbances of the summer. Among its reforms were the transformation of local government, which included the substitution of departments for the old provinces and a new system of law courts; the seizure of the ecclesiastical lands; the abolition of the nobility; and the reorganisation of the French Church. Though never holding office, the dominant personality was Mirabeau, whose death in April 1791 weakened relations between Louis XVI and the Assembly. These were further worsened by the flight to Varennes and the Declaration of Pilnitz, both of which encouraged the growth of republicanism in the country.

VI In political terms, this period resulted in the replacement of the monarchy by the republic and in social terms the challenge to the middle-class notables by the sans-culottes, the Parisian militants who wore trousers and not the knee-breeches of polite society. The coming of war immediately placed the king in a false position. He was now a monarch with a limited role in the government of the country engaged in a struggle to preserve the new state against enemies whose avowed purpose was to restore the powers he had previously possessed over his subjects. The passions aroused by the situation brought to an end the brief experiment of constitutional monarchy. It also brought to an end the constructive stage of the Revolution. It had now little more to achieve by way of a permanent contribution to French history.

VII M. J. Sydenham, *The Girondins* (1961), has shown that they were too small to be a real party and had no political programme. They were no more than a faction, a small, individualistic group of friends, many of whom came from the region of the Gironde, around Bordeaux. They wanted power. The outbreak of war in 1792 had brought them this, and they had managed to retain it in the National Convention. They were unable, however, to deal with the deteriorating military situation and serious economic difficulties from early in 1793, and they never had the support of Paris. They feared the Jacobin appeal to the masses, but when they belatedly attempted to arrest the Jacobin leaders, they themselves were overthrown. M. J. Sydenham has commented, 'Their complete independence as individuals is demonstrably the real reason for their complete failure to govern France'.

VIII There has been much discussion about the nature and origins of the Terror. What has been called the 'thesis of circumstance' holds that it came about as a result of the threats of war to the Republic. On the other hand, it has been suggested that the course of the Revolution was marked by increasing violence and hatred and that the Terror was a culmination implicit in the nature of the movement itself. The character of Robespierre himself has also been subjected to assessment and reassessment – was he tyrannical and bloodthirsty, a figurehead dominated by others or an unsuccessful social reformer? As J. M. Roberts has said, 'The reputation of Robespierre provides something of a touchstone of the political use of the Revolution even down to the present day'.

The Revolution has traditionally been regarded as ending with

Robespierre's downfall in 1794. There has recently been a greater interest in Post-Thermidorian politics, and the final extracts in this chapter suggest the course it took.

I The Failure of Reform under Louis XVI

Introduction

The French monarchy reached the climax of its power during the reign of Louis XIV, but by the time of his death in 1715 serious signs of weakness were appearing, and three-quarters of a century later it was brought down through revolution. The threat to the kingdom was recognised by many people, who realised also that it could only be avoided by drastic changes. They failed, and this chapter looks at the reason (in Alfred Cobban's words) 'why reform had to give place to revolution'. It considers five aspects of the problem, as it appeared to contemporaries, French and foreign, during the reign of Louis XVI, the last king of the *ancien régime*, showing what fears and aspirations it aroused among them, and what solutions they advocated or opposed. These sections are separate and different, but together they give an insight into the situation in France during the critical period of thirty years:

1 The characters of Louis XVI and Marie Antoinette were inevitably of importance during this period. Louis XIV had established at Versailles a monarchy which governed France personally and a court which was the centre of French power and culture, but it required his successors to be able and willing to make it effective. Louis XV was unequal to this. Louis XVI was even more inadequate, and his queen made the position worse.

2 The estates of France were the clergy, the nobility and the third estate, the three medieval orders of society into which the kingdom was divided. Among the clergy, there was a deep social division. At the outbreak of the Revolution, only 1 of the 130 bishops was not a nobleman, while the lower clergy belonged to the middle classes and peasantry. The nobility were divided into the old *noblesse d'epée*, who depended upon court posts or military service, and the new *noblesse de robe*, who entered the landowning class and exploited their privileges and feudal dues. This *réaction seigneuriale* aroused growing resentment from members of the third estate.

3 The European intellectual movement, the Enlightenment, strongly influenced the French reformers. The extracts in this section illustrate some of the ideas of its thinkers, the philosophes, and the opposition they met.

4 France during this period faced serious financial and economic difficulties. Anne-Robert Turgot, who was Controller-General of Finances from 1774 to 1776, temporarily secured some reforms, persuading Louis XVI to issue decrees implementing them. The extracts here include, as examples, the edict suppressing the guilds, and the controversy over another reform, the abolition of the corvée, which Jacques Necker, his successor, later supported. Opposition to reform came largely from the parlements, the sovereign courts of justice, which rejected royal edicts. These had become strongholds of the new nobility and were determined to preserve their power and privileges.

5 Finally, the French attitude towards Britain and the United States of America was important during these years. These countries aroused admiration and emulation in France, but also resentment at the continual failure of French foreign policy, which Napoleon thought was an important cause of the Revolution.

1 The King and Queen

(a) *Louis XVI's brother-in-law, the Emperor Joseph II, in 1777*

This man is a little feeble, but not at all an imbecile; he has ideas and judgement, but suffers from an apathy of both body and will. While he converses reasonably, he has neither curiosity nor a wish to inform himself. In short, the *fiat lux* has not yet come, the matter has
5   not yet been formed into the globe.

> *Correspondance secrète entre Marie-Thérèse et le Comte de Mercy-Argentau avec les lettres de Marie-Thérèse et de Marie-Antoinette* (eds A. d'Arneth and A. Geffroy, 3 vols, 1875), III, p 74n

(b) *The Abbé de Véri in 1775*

The king is seen passing his mornings in his closet observing with his telescope those who arrive at Versailles. He often occupies himself in sweeping, nailing and unnailing. Some common sense, simple tastes, an honest heart, a sound conscience, that is his good side. A
10   tendency to indecision, a weak will, abilities limited by his manner of perceiving and apprehending: there is the contrast.

> L'Abbé de Véri, *Journal* (ed. J. de Witte, 2 vols, 1929), I, p 244

(c) *A contemporary in 1787*

His Majesty's physical condition requires him to take plenty of exercise. Endowed with unusual strength, his appetite matches his powers. This is the menu for one of his usual breakfasts. At six
15   o'clock the king rises and asks what there is for breakfast. 'Sire, a fat chicken and chops.' – 'It would be easy to poach me some eggs in

meat juice.' The king supervises the preparations, eats four chops, the fat chicken, six eggs in meat juice and a slice of ham and drinks a bottle and a half of champagne; he dresses, sets out to hunt and returns with an incredible appetite.

> *Correspondance secrète inédite sur Louis XVI, Marie-Antoinette, la cour et la ville de 1777 à 1792* (ed. M. F. A. de Lescure, 2 vols, 1866), II, p 151

(d) A member of the parlement of Paris

Louis XVI was exempt from the vices which spring from strong emotions, but he also lacked the energy to which they give birth. Nature, having given him the amiability and the virtues pleasing in a private individual, denied him the qualities needed by one destined to command. His education had done little to remedy the defects of his nature. Timidity and mistrust of himself were at the centre of his character; and it was soon recognized that, if he were not to be guided by his own inclinations, others could succeed by skill and perseverance in influencing his decisions.

> Guy-Marie Sallier, *Annales françaises depuis le commencement du règne de Louis XVI jusqu'aux Etats Généraux de 1774 à 1789* (1813), pp 5–6

(e) The Duc de Levis

The nobility, coming to realize that it was foolish to make a long journey merely in order to secure an ungracious reception, preferred to stay at home. . . . Versailles, a scene of such magnificence in the days of Louis XIV, when all Europe was eager to come thither for lessons in good taste and good manners, now became nothing more than a minor provincial town which one visited with nonchalance and left with alacrity.

> Gaston, Duc de Levis, *Souvenirs et Portraits* (1813), p 26

(f) The Austrian ambassador (Marie Antoinette's mentor) to her mother, Maria Theresa, in 1776

Among the rumours which circulate contrary to the prestige and reputation essential to a queen of France, there is one which appears more dangerous and unpleasant than the rest. . . . It is complained quite openly that the queen is extravagant and encourages extravagance.

The public at first viewed with pleasure the king's gift of the Trianon to the queen; but it began to be disturbed and alarmed by H.M.'s expenditure there. By her order the gardens have been completely changed into an English garden, which cost at least 150,000 livres. The queen has had a theatre built at the Trianon; she has only presented one play there followed by a supper, but this entertainment was very expensive. . . .

50   The queen's allowance has been doubled, and yet she has contracted debts. . . . The chief cause of the queen's debts is known and excites no fewer outcries and complaints. The queen has brought many diamonds, and her card-playing has become very costly; she no longer plays at games of commerce, in which the loss is necessarily limited. Lansquenet [in which the players bet on single

55   cards] has become her usual game, and sometimes faro [in which the players bet on the order in which certain cards will appear], when she is not playing in full public view. The ladies and courtiers are dismayed and distressed by the losses to which they expose themselves in order to make their court to the queen.

Correspondance secrète entre Marie-Thérèse . . ., II, pp 493–7

(g) The British chargé d'affaires in Paris

60   It is to the court, my lord, that you must look for the sources of the present evil. The Queen, not only during the latter years of the reign of the late King, but even till after the birth of the Dauphin, by which event the succession seemed in some measure secured, was very far from enjoying that degree of power and influence which she is

65   possessed of at present. But that event decided all the courtiers, and they hastened with precipitation to the standard of favour; while those who had before constituted Her Majesty's intimate and circumscribed society were soon consolidated with a formidable party in the State. The strong propensity of the Princess to every

70   kind of pleasure and expense has been improved into great advantage by all those who have considered only their elevation and advancement. Her pretended friends, by administering to her pleasures, are become the intimate participators of her secrets, and, having once got possession of them, they may, in fact, be said to be

75   masters of their own mistress, and to have secured by that means to themselves the permanence of that power, which otherwise the changeableness of her disposition rendered extremely precarious. . . .

The voice of the people is now and then, indeed, faintly heard in

80   their remonstrances, but as the avenues to the throne are all secured by the profusion of the Minister to all who are in credit and power, it has little or no effect and dies away for want of being seconded. I know it has been said that the extent of the influence of the Queen's party goes no further than to the disposal of certain places and

85   pensions without interfering with the great line of public business, and particularly that of foreign affairs, but it ought surely to be observed, that, when any set of them can command the person who holds the purse of the State, they must necessarily have the greatest

direct influence in all internal and a considerable indirect share in all
foreign affairs.

Daniel Hales to Lord Carmarthen, 25 October 1786, *Despatches from Paris 1784–1790* (ed. Oscar Browning, Camden Society, Third Series), vol XVI, p 145

(h) The Duc de Levis

In an age of pleasure and frivolity, intoxicated with supreme power,
the queen had no fancy for submitting herself to constraint, and she
found the court ceremonies tedious. . . . She thought it absurd to
suppose that the loyalty of the common people could depend upon
the number of hours which the royal family spent in a circle of bored
and boring courtiers. . . . Except for a few favourites, chosen for
some whim or because of a successful intrigue, everyone was
excluded from the royal presence.

Gaston, Duc de Levis, op cit, p 54

Questions

a In what ways were Louis XVI and Marie Antoinette unequal to
the position they inherited?
b What encouraged factions at the court?
c How had the importance of the court of Versailles declined since
the reign of Louis XIV?
★ *d* To what extent was the idea of excessive royal expenditure due to
anti-monarchical propaganda?

2 The Estates

(a) The higher clergy

How wicked are those parents who force their children into the
Church merely in the family interest. Has nature made the heart of a
younger son more pure and more inclined to fulfil those sacred and
sublime duties of the priesthood than those of his brother? . . . And
so, my brethren, in order not to divide your goods, you sacrifice
your children and the fruit of your loins. A sacred calling, which we
did not expect, strips us in an instant of all worldly dross and bears
one into the holy place, when lo! the death of an elder brother
changes all our views, hurls us back into the world we have left, and
our vocation for the altar dwindles as now earthly hopes spring up in
our hearts. Barbarous and inhuman parents count it as nothing to
sacrifice all their other sons and thrust them into the abyss in order to
raise one of their sons to a position above that of his ancestors, and
thus make him the idol of their vanity. My God! how terrible for
those unnatural parents will be the presence of their unhappy victims
on the Day of Judgement! And may the horror of their fate appeal to

Your Justice to avenge their blood on the authors of their being and of their eternal misfortune!

Jean-Baptiste Massillon, Bishop of Clermont, 'Sermon de Vocations', *Oeuvres Complêtes* (1832), p 28

(b) The lower clergy

None are so wretched and so oppressed as the lower clergy. While
20 the Bishop plays the great nobleman and spends scandalous sums on hounds, horses, furniture, servants, food and carriages, the parish priest has not the wherewithal to buy himself a new cassock. The burden of collecting the tithe falls on him, but the Prelates, not he, pocket it. The Bishops treat their priests, not as honest footmen,
25 but as stable-boys.

L'Abbé Michel Lavassor, *Les Soupirs de la France Esclavé, qui aspire après la liberté*, in L. Ducros, *French Society in the Eighteenth Century* (trans. W. de Geijer, 1926), pp 281–2

(c) The unpopularity of the nobility

The castles, which bristle in our provinces and swallow up large estates, possess misused rights of hunting, fishing and cutting wood; and these castles still conceal those haughty gentlemen who separate themselves effectively from the human race, who add their own
30 taxes to those of the monarch, and who oppress all too easily the poor, despondent peasant, even if they have lost the privilege of killing him and casting ten pounds on his grave.

The rest of the nobility surround the throne, their hands continually open to beg eternally for pensions and places. They want
35 everything for themselves – dignities, employments and exclusive preferences; they will not allow the common people to have either promotion or reward, whatever their ability or their services to their country; they forbid them to serve by land or sea; then they want bishoprics, abbacies and benefices, for all those who do not want to
40 serve.

L. S. Mercier, *Tableau de Paris* (12 vols, 1783–9), VIII, p 154

(d) The old and new nobility

What spectacle more affecting to behold for gentlemen of old extraction, often returned to their lands with honourable marks of their services and their courage, than to see at every turn their escutcheons mingled with those of persons who have barely had
45 time to buy the right to possess them, and to find themselves compelled at church to share with those newcomers the honours which for several centuries have been rendered only to them [the real gentlemen] and their ancestors.

Remonstrance du Parlement de Paris (1748) in Franklin L. Ford, *Robe and Sword* (1965), p 198

(e) The younger nobility

Without regret for the past, without anxiety for the future, we young nobles walked light-heartedly on the carpet of flowers which concealed us from an abyss. We were smiling mockers of the ancient ways, the feudal pride of our fathers and their grave etiquettes, and everything that was old was boring and ridiculous to us. The gravity of the old-fashioned doctrines was too burdensome for us. The smiling philosophy of Voltaire attracted us, because it was so amusing. Without deeply inquiring into the thought of the more serious writers, we admired it because it was instinct with courage and opposition to arbitrary power. . . .

We were inclined to surrender whole-heartedly to the philosophical doctrines put forward by men of letters, who were so witty and bold. Voltaire seduced our minds; Rousseau touched our hearts; we took secret pleasure in the fact that these men attacked the old edifice that seemed to us to be Gothic and ridiculous. So, whatever might be the rank and privileges we held as the survival of our former power, which we being undermined at that very moment, we took pleasure in this little war; for we did not feel its dangers, we only saw it as a piece of drama. . . .

We laughed at the solemn fears of the old Court and the Clergy, who thundered against this spirit of innovation. We applauded the republican plays at the theatre, the philosophical discourses at the Academy and the daring books of our men of letters. . . . The idea of Liberty, in whatever way it was expressed, pleased us by its courage, its spirit of equality and its general convenience. Men find it a pleasure to stoop below themselves, as long as they can feel able to rise up again whenever they please; and since we did not look far ahead, we were able to sample at one and the same time the advantages of aristocracy and the luxury of a plebian philosophy.

Louis-Philippe, Comte de Ségur, *Memoires ou Souvenirs et Anecdotes* (3 vols, 1826), I, p 203

(f) The third estate

What does a nation need to live and prosper? – private enterprise and public undertakings.

Private enterprise can be divided into four classes –

1. The oceans and the fertile land make possible the production of the basic means of satisfying man's needs, so the first class are all the families who work in the country or at sea.

2. From the first selling of this produce for its consumption or use, further handiwork adds a second value to it. So human industry sets out to perfect the benefits of nature and increases their value two, ten or a hundredfold. These are the achievements of the second class of enterprise.

3. Between production and consumption, as well as between the

90   different processes of production, there are many that are intermediate and beneficial to both producers and consumers. They are
carried out by the merchants who, ceaselessly calculating the needs of
time and space, seek their profit by marketing and transport-
ing the produce, and the vendors, who engage in wholesale or retail
95   transactions. This type of useful activity characterizes the third class.
        4. Besides these three classes of industrious and useful citizens,
who occupy themselves with the business of consumption and
employment, there also has to be in a Society a multitude of private
workers, who care directly for the needs or comfort of the people.
100   This fourth class ranges from the scientific and liberal professions,
which are the most distinguished, to domestic service, which is the
least esteemed.
        Such are the labours which sustain Society. Who undertakes
them? – the Third Estate.
105   Public undertakings similarly comprise four recognized classes –
the Sword, the Robe, the Church and the Government. It would be
unnecessary to consider them in detail to show that the Third Estate
together forms nineteen-twentieths of those who serve Society,
with this difference, it is engaged in everything that is truly
110   laborious, in all the duties that the privileged Order refuses to
undertake. Lucrative and honorific positions are only occupied by
members of the privileged Order.

> Emmanuel-Joseph Sieyès, *Qu'est-ce que le Tiers-Etat?* (Second
> Edition, 1789), pp 5–7

(g) *The ambitions of the lawyers*

The privileges of the nobility are truly their property. We will
respect them all the more because we are not excluded from them
115   and because we can acquire them: great actions, gallantry, courage,
personal merits, offices, fortune even, all these are paths that lead us
to them. Why, then, suppose that we might think of destroying the
source of emulation which guides our labours?

> *Lettre des avocats de Nuits en Bourgogne, 31 December 1788* in
> Douglas Johnson (ed.), *French Society and the Revolution*
> (1976), p 123

Questions

a   To what extent does extract *a* account for the social gulf between
    the higher and lower clergy described in extract *b*?
b   'The French nobility were divided deeply in origins, way of life
    and outlook'. Consider this statement with reference to extracts
    c, *d* and *e*.
c   How did the ideas of Sieyès about political power differ from
    those of the *ancien régime*?
★ d   How far was it possible for members of the third estate to raise
    themselves to the ranks of the *noblesse de robe*?

3 The Enlightenment

(a) A defence of the philosophes

Our century enjoys a great advantage over former times in having such a great number of educated men who pass from the thorns of mathematics to the flowers of poetry and judge equally well a book of metaphysics and a play. The spirit of the century has made most of them as much at ease in society as in their study. This is the great advantage they hold over men of letters of preceding centuries. Up to the time of Balzac and Voiture they were not admitted to society; since that time they have become a necessary part of it. The profound and clear reasoning which many have infused into their books and their conversation has done much to instruct and polish the nation. Their criticism is no longer spent on Greek and Latin works, but, with the aid of a sound philosophy, it has destroyed all the prejudices with which society was afflicted: astrologers' predictions, the divinings of magicians, all types of witchcraft, false prodigies, false marvels and superstitious customs. This philosophy has relegated to the schools thousands of childish disputations which had formerly been dangerous and have now become objects of scorn. In this way men of letters have, in fact, served the state. We are sometimes dismayed that matters which formerly disturbed the world no longer trouble it to-day. We owe this to true men of letters.

L'Encyclopédie (1751–72), article 'Hommes de Lettres' by F. M. A. de Voltaire

(b) Another defence of the philosophes

Our philosopher does not count himself an exile in the world; he does not suppose himself in the enemy's country he would fain find pleasure with others, and to find it he must give it; he is a worthy man who wishes to please and make himself useful. The ordinary philsophers, who meditate too much, or rather who meditate to wrong purpose, are as surly and arrogant to all people as great people are to those whom they do not think their equals; they flee men, and men avoid them. But our philosopher, who knows how to divide himself between retreat and the commerce of men, is full of humanity. Civil society is, so to say, a divinity for him on the earth; he honours it by his probity, by an exact attention to his duties and by a sincere desire not to be a useless or embarrassing member of it. The sage has the leaven of order and rule: he is full of ideas connected with the good of civil society. What experience shows us every day is that the more reason and light people have, the better fitted they are and the more to be relied on for the common intercourse of life.

Denis Diderot, Pensées philosophiques (1746) in Kingsley Martin, French Liberal Thought in the Eighteenth Century (1962), p 92

(c) An attack on the philosophes

Hatred, jealousy and destruction contain the whole science of the pretended sages. Hate the Gospel, calumniate its author, overthrow his altars, and your science will be that of the modern
40 Philosopher. Profess yourself a Deist, an Atheist, a Sceptic, a Spinozist, in short, whatever you please; deny or affirm, set up a doctrine or a worship in opposition to the religion of Christ, or set up none, that is not what . . . Voltaire requires to constitute a model Philosopher. When asked what doctrine he wished to substitute to
45 that of Christ, he did not think himself authorized to answer. 'I have delivered them from the physicians (he called the clergy physicians), what farther service do they require?' Require! Have you not infected them with the plague? Have you not unbridled every passion? And what remedies have you left them? In vain were it for
50 us to challenge Voltaire and panegyrist Condorcet; they will not answer. – No, follow their example; declare all religious truths to be erroneous, false or popular prejudices, to be superstition or fanaticism; glory in destruction, little troubling yourself with substituting science for ignorance or truth for error; to have
55 destroyed will suffice, and for that you shall be entitled to the high-sounding name of a modern Philosopher. . . .

Whatever may have been the causes, it was ordained that an age deceived by the intrigues and conspiracies of impiety should glory in styling itself the *Age of Philosophy*. It was ordained that an age, a dupe
60 to the frantic rage of impiety substituted for reason, a dupe to the oaths of hatred and the wish of crushing all religion mistaken for toleration, religious liberty and equality, to ignorance for science, to depravity for virtue, a dupe in short to all the intrigues and plots of the most profound wickedness mistaken for the methods and
65 achievements of wisdom; it was ordained, I say, that this *Age of Philosophy* should also be dupes to the plots of the rebellious Sophisters, mistaken for the love of society and the basis of public happiness.

The conspiracy against the altar, the hatred sworn by the chiefs
70 against their God, were not the only legacies bequeathed by the chiefs to this school of modern philosophy. Voltaire was the father of the Sophisters of Modern Impiety, and before his death he became the chief of the Sophisters of Rebellion. He said to his first adepts, 'Let us crush the altar and let not a single altar nor a single worshipper
75 be left to the God of the Christians.' And his school soon resounded with the cry of, '*Let us crush the sceptre* and let not a single throne nor a single subject be left to the kings of the earth!' It was from the mutual success of these two schools that the revolution was to be generated in France, which, grasping the hatchet, was at the same time to
80 destroy the altar of the living God and imbue its steps with the blood of its pontiffs; to overthrow the throne and strike off the head of the

unfortunate Louis XVI, menacing all the altars of Christendom, all the kings of the earth with a similar fate. To the plots contrived under the veil of liberty and equality, applied to *religion*, and of religious toleration, are to succeed those begotten under the veil of *political* liberty and equality.

> L'Abbé Augustin Barruel, *Memoirs Illustrating the History of Jacobinism* (2 vols, 1799), I, pp 224–5

(d) Freedom of the press upheld

In general, it is as natural a right to use one's pen as one's tongue with its perils, risks and fortunes. I know many books that are boring; I do not know any that have done any real evil. Theologians or so-called statesmen cry, 'Religion is destroyed, government is lost, if you print certain truths or certain paradoxes. You must only think after having requested a license from a monk or a clerk. It is contrary to good order that a man should think independently. Homer, Plato, Cicero, Virgil, Pliny, Horace never published anything without the approval of the doctors of the Sorbonne and the Holy Inquisition.

See into what horrible decadence freedom of the press has cast England and Holland. It is true that they control the trade of the whole world, and that England is victorious at sea and on land; but this is only a false grandeur, a false opulence; they advance rapidly towards their ruin. An enlightened people cannot endure.'

One cannot reason more justly, my friends; now let us see, if you please, how the State has been endangered by a book. The most dangerous, the most pernicious of all that is that of Spinoza. Not only as a Jew does he attack the New Testament, but as a scholar he destroys Antiquity; his system of atheism is more attractive, more reasonable than that of Epicurius. . . .

I detest like you this book, which I understand perhaps better than you, and to which you have responded with alarm; but have you seen that this book has changed the face of the world? Is there any priest who has lost a florin of his stipend by the sale of Spinoza's works? Is there a bishop whose income has diminished? On the contrary, their revenue has doubled since that time. All the harm is confined to a small number of peaceful professors, who have examined Spinoza's arguments in their study, and who have written for or against these little-known works. . . .

Oh, you say to me, the books of Luther and Calvin destroyed the Roman religion and part of Europe. . . . No, Rome was not conquered by books. It was because it drove Europe to revolt by its plundering, by the public sale of indulgences, by degrading men, by wishing to govern them like domestic animals, by abusing its power so excessively that it is astonishing that it preserved a single village.

> F. M. A. de Voltaire, *Dictionnaire philosophique* (1764), article 'Liberté d'imprimer'

(e) Freedom of the press contradicted

The multiplicity of contentious or licentious writings in a nation is almost always either the sign of decadence or the forewarning of a revolution.

125 In a country where the citizens exercise the greater part of legislative power, the freedom of the press has its limits and produces disorders there when it exceeds the bounds that it ought to observe. It has to be restrained, therefore, by the constitution.

In monarchies, however, where the power is more concentrated
130 and where the government's decisions are by their nature more secret, permission to print, if readily granted, causes grave trouble and even becomes dangerous, if that power, which the law ought always to have to repress the abuse, is restrained; and even though it may be hoped that anonymous writers confine themselves within
135 the terms of an exact impartiality, is it a good thing ceaselessly to reveal wrongs without being able to show precisely any remedies, to persuade the citizen that the laws under which he lives, under which his fathers have lived, are unjust and barbarous, that his customs are senseless, when in their place are only offered dreams, sometimes
140 attractive in theory but always impossible to put into effect, because all such plans are imperfect, when practical knowledge is lacking, and a newly-devised constitution is offered instead of the genius and morals of a nation, above all, that way of life which peoples hold from tradition, and which it is dangerous to check or alter too
145 abruptly?

Thus the poison progresses rapidly, ideas become distorted, opinions spread, parties gain converts, and soon the citizen grows restless under the hand which governs him; he criticizes one by one all the laws which he has hitherto respected, and it is not difficult to
150 realize that when one comes to despise them, the next step is to disobey them. Often also the argument inflames people's minds and colours their imaginations; what was only an opinion becomes an accepted belief with its precepts, its tendencies and its consequences.

When the word of liberty was heard for the first time, it proposed
155 only to remove some restrictions on means of communication; it cannot be doubted that it will soon strike at all aspects of the government. A vague criticism of the temporal authority of the papacy, a bitter satire on the abuses of the clergy, these were the first steps that two centuries ago led to the unhappy schisms, which
160 divided the Roman Church and shed so much blood throughout Europe.

Remonstrance du Parlement de Paris, 18 April 1776, Albert Bayet and Francois Albert (eds), *Les Ecrivains politiques du XVIII siècle* (1926), pp 424–5

(f) The political economy of the physiocrats

The social laws, established by the Supreme Being, prescribe firmly the upholding of the right of property and of liberty which are inseparable.

The ordinances of sovereigns, which are termed positive laws, should only be acts setting forth those laws essential for this social order.

If the ordinances of sovereigns are contrary to the laws of the social order, if they fail to respect property, if they order the destruction of crops, if they countenance the sacrifice of children, they are not laws, they are insensitive acts which no one is bound to obey.

There is, then, a natural and unexceptionable arbiter of these laws of sovereigns, and this arbiter is the evidence of their conformity or their opposition to the laws of the social order.

The laws to which we rightly owe the utmost respect and complete obedience are those which benefit everyone, and those to which men are bound to submit by the religion of their conscience, even when they are not promulgated by the sovereign, and when he does not employ all the power of his legal authority to enforce them.

Dupont de Nemours, *Origine et Progrès d'une Science Nouvelle* (1768), ibid, p 335

(g) Its alleged consequences

To all the enemies of God and His Christ, I add another sect known under the name of economists. These men, disciples of Turgot, for thirty years tormented France, claiming to reform its government and restore its finances by schemes which ruined its monarchy and wasted its treasure. All the science of these sophists was contained in what they called the 'clear consequences'; and the 'clear consequences' of their dogmas required the destruction of every aspect of Christianity to substitute for it the practice of a religion which they call natural, just as the 'clear consequences' of their expedients to enrich the nation led them to rob the altar and slaughter its priests.

L'Abbé Augustin Barruel, *Histoire de Clergé pendant la Révolution française* (1793), pp 6–7

Questions

a How did Voltaire and Diderot in extracts *a* and *b* seek to prove that the philosophes were valuable and useful members of society?

b Which do you think more convincing – Voltaire's arguments for the freedom of the press in extract *d* or those of the Parlement of Paris against it in extract *e*?

c   Why did the Abbé Barruel in extracts *c* and *g* consider that the
    ideas of the philsophes and physiocrats were anti-Christian?
★ d   'A time-bomb set to destroy the French kingdom.' Do you agree
    with this description of the Enlightenment?

4   The Weaknesses and Abuses of the Kingdom

(a) *Turgot's financial programme*

No bankruptcy.
No increase of taxation.
No loans.
No bankruptcy, either open or concealed by compulsory
5 reductions of interest.
No increase of taxation, which is demanded by the condition of
the people and even more by Your Majesty's goodness of heart.
No loans, because every loan must reduce the revenue actually at
our disposal; at the end of a certain time it means either bankruptcy
10 or increasing taxes. In peacetime we must only borrow to liquidate
former debts or to redeem other loans made at a higher rate of
interest.
There is only one way of achieving these three points. It is to make
our expenses lower than our debts, low enough to be able to save
15 each year twenty million, in order to pay off old debts. Without this,
the first cannon-shot will force the State into bankruptcy.
Mémoire au Roi, 24 August 1774, *Oeuvres de Turgot* (ed.
G. Schelle, 5 vols, 1913–23), IV, pp 109–10

(b) *Freedom of labour*

God, in making man dependent upon the necessities of life, so that he
has to work, has made the right to work the possession of all men,
and this possession is the first, the most sacred and the most
20 inalienable of all.
We consider that one of the first duties of our justice and one of the
worthiest acts of our beneficence is to free our subjects from all the
constraints imposed upon this permanent right of humanity. We
wish consequently to abrogate these arbitrary institutions which do
25 not allow the needy to live by their work; which restrict a sex whose
weakness has given her more needs and less resources, and which
appear, in condemning her to inevitable wretchedness, to assist
seduction and debauchery; which discourage competition and
industry and render useless the talents of those whose circumstances
30 exclude them from membership of a guild; which deprive the State
and the arts of all the skills which foreigners bring; which retard the
progress of the arts by the numerous difficulties facing inventors

when different guilds dispute the right to put into effect the discoveries which they themselves have not made; which, by the heavy fees that workmen have to pay to acquire permission to work, by the exactions of every sort imposed upon them, by the numerous fines for alleged offences, by expenses and waste of all sort, by the endless law-suits undertaken by all guilds to uphold their respective claims to their exclusive privileges, imposing upon industry a huge burden oppressive to its subjects without any gain for the State; which, finally, by the encouragement which they give to the members of the guilds to accept uniform conditions, to compel the poorest members to submit to the law of the rich, becoming an instrument of monopoly and favouring policies which have the effect of increasing beyond their natural level the prices of the necessities of the people.

Edit du Roi, portant suppression des jurands, 1774, Bayet and Albert, op cit, pp 348–9

(c) *Turgot's political criticism*

The cause of evil, Sire, comes from the fact that your nation has no constitution. It is a society composed of badly-ordered ranks and a people whose members have only a few social links between them; where consequently each person is occupied with little more than his own exclusive interest, hardly anyone troubles to fulfil his duties or consider his obligations towards others; consequently, in this perpetual war of claims and actions, which mutual reason and understanding have never regulated, Your Majesty is obliged to decide everything by himself or by his confidants. Your detailed orders are needed to contribute towards the public well-being, to uphold the rights of others, sometime even to use one's own property. You are forced to legislate upon everything and usually by particular decrees, whereas you could govern like God by general laws, if the integral groups of your kingdom had a regular form of government and known relationships.

Mémoire au Roi sur les Municipalités, 1776, Bayet and Albert, op cit, pp 364–5

(d) *Support for the corvée*

In relieving from the corvée the lowest class of citizens, who have so far been subject to it, the edict imposes the tax on the two orders of the State who have never been liable to it.

There are no longer any distinctions between all your subjects; the nobility and the clergy become liable to the corvée or, which is the same thing, have to replace the tax which is to replace the corvée.

This is not, as we have sought to persuade you, Sire, a contest between the rich and the poor.

70   It is a question of State and one of the most important, because it is
raised to determine if all your subjects can and should be mingled
together, if it is desirable to cease to recognize among them different
conditions of ranks, titles and pre-eminences.

To subject the nobility to a tax for redeeming the corvée, contrary
75   to the maxim that 'no one is subject to the corvée if he is not liable to
the taille,' is to decide that they are liable to the corvée like
commoners; and once this principle is admitted, they could be
subject to the personal corvée whenever it was re-imposed. . . .

What, indeed, can reassure the nobility that, after they have been
80   made liable to the corvée, it is not intended later to impose the taille
upon them?

Would it be less difficult to close the immense gap which separates
their position from that of the former serfs than that which separates
them from citizens who are freeborn, though commoners?
85   No, without a doubt.

Once the first barrier has been broken, the second will be
overthrown much more easily.

Rémonstrance du Parlement de Paris, 2 March 1776, ibid,
pp 422–3

(e) The iniquity of the corvée

I can only say that the more I examine this important question, the
more I am convinced that means should be adopted to abolish the
90   corvée. This matter is, in the last analysis, nothing else than a contest
between rich and poor, because it is easy to see at once the advantages
the poor would gain from the suppression of the corvée. A man
without resources, a wage-earner, from whom is exacted seven or
eight days corvée-labour, would only have to pay twelve or fifteen
95   sous for his share of the road-tax, if this was assessed with the taille,
and he would still be able to recover fully the cost of this small
contribution by the introduction of new projects with paid labour,
the benefit of which he could share by working on them. There is no
doubt, then, that the corvée is clearly contrary to the interests of this
100   class of your subjects, towards whom the bountiful hand of Your
Majesty ought ceaselesssly to extend in order to relieve, as much as
possible, the overbearing yoke imposed upon them by men of
property and wealth.

Compte Rendu au Roi par M. Necker au mois de Janvier 1781
(1781), pp 69–70

(f) The perversion of justice

The administration of justice was partial, venal, infamous. I have, in
105   conversation with many very sensible men, in different parts of the
kingdom, met with something of content with their government, in
all respécts than this; but upon the question of expecting justice to be

really and fairly administered, everyone confessed that there was no such thing to be looked for. The conduct of the parliaments was profligate and atrocious. Upon almost every cause that came before them, interest was openly made with the judges; and woe betided the man who, with a cause to support, had no means of conciliating favour, either by the beauty of a handsome wife or by other methods. It has been said, by many writers, that property was as secure under the old government of France as it is in England; and the assertion might possibly be true, as far as any violence from the King, his ministers or the great was concerned; but for all that large amount of property, which comes in every country to be litigated in courts of justice, there was not even the shadow of security, unless the parties were totally and unequally unknown and totally and equally honest; in every other case, he who had the best interest with the judges was sure to be the winner. To reflecting minds, the cruelty and abominable practice attending such courts are sufficiently apparent. There was also a circumstance in the constitution of these parliaments but little known in England, and which, under such a government as that of France, must be considered as very singular. They had the power and were in constant practice of issuing decrees, without the consent of the Crown, and which had the force of laws through the whole of their jurisdiction; and of all other laws, these were sure to be the best obeyed; for as all infringements were brought before sovereign courts, composed of the same persons who had enacted these laws (a horrible system of tyranny) they were certain of being punished with the last severity.

Arthur Young, *Travels in France during the Years 1787, 1788 and 1789* (ed. Constantia Maxwell, 1950), pp 333–4

Questions

a   Was French fiscal inefficiency responsible for Turgot's desire for the reforms outlined in extract *a*?
b   What were (i) the 'corvée' (line 62) and (ii) the 'taille' (line 95)?
c   What do these extracts reveal about the nature of the *despotisme légale* of the French monarchy?
d   'They had been bourgeois and royalist; they became noble, feudal, factious.' (Joseph Barnave, 1789). Discuss this description of the development of the parlements during the eighteenth century.

5   British and American Influences

(a) Voltaire on England, 1726–29

The power of the House of Commons has increased every day. The families of the ancient peers are at last extinct; and as peers only are properly noble in England, there would be no such thing in strictness of law in that island, had not the kings created new barons from time to time and preserved the body of peers, once a terror to them, to oppose them to the Commons, since become so formidable.

All these new peers, who compose the Higher House, receive nothing but their titles from the king, and very few of them have estates in those places whence they take their titles. One shall be Duke of D_____, though he has not a foot of land in Dorsetshire; and another is Earl of a village, though he scarce knows where it is situated. The peers have power, but it is only in the Parliament House.

There is no such thing here as *haute, moyenne* and *basse justice* – that is, a power to judge in all matters civil and criminal; nor a right or privilege of hunting in the grounds of a citizen, who at the same time is not permitted to fire a gun in his own field.

No one is exempted in this country from paying certain taxes because he is a nobleman or a priest. All duties and taxes are settled by the House of Commons, whose power is greater than that of the Peers, though inferior to it in dignity. The spiritual as well as temporal Lords have the power to reject a Money Bill brought in by the Commons; but they are not allowed to alter anything in it and must either pass or throw it out without restriction. When the Bill has passed the Lords and is signed by the king, then the whole nation pays, every man in proportion to his revenue or estate, not according to his title, which would be absurd. There is no such thing as an arbitrary subsidy or poll-tax, but a real tax on the lands, of all which an estimate was made in the reign of the famous King William III.

The land-tax continues still upon the same foot, though the revenue of the lands is increased. Thus no one is tyrannised over, and everyone is easy. The feet of the peasants are not bruised by wooden shoes; they eat white bread, are well clothed and are not afraid of increasing their cattle, nor of tiling their houses, from any apprehension that their taxes will be raised the year following. The annual income of the estates of a great many commoners in England amounts to two hundred thousand livres, and yet these do not think it beneath them to plough their lands which enrich them, and on which they enjoy their liberty.

H. Morley (ed.), *Voltaire's Letters on England* (1889), Letter IX 'On Government'

(b) The American War of Independence

Soon the American envoys, Silas Deane and Arthur Lee, arrived in Paris, and shortly afterwards the famous Benjamin Franklin joined them. It would be difficult to express the enthusiasm and fervour with which they were welcomed in France, into the midst of an old monarchy – these envoys of a people in insurrection against their king. Nothing could be more striking than the contrast between the luxury of our capital, the elegance of our fashions, the magnificence of Versailles, the polished but haughty arrogance of our nobles – in short all those living signs of the monarchical pride of Louis XIV – with the utmost rustic dress, the simple if proud demeanour, the frank, direct speech, the plain, unpowdered hair and finally that flavour of antiquity which seemed to bring suddenly within our walls and into the midst of the soft and servile civilization of the seventeenth century these sage contemporaries of Plato or republicans of Cato's or Fabius's time.

> Louis-Philippe, Comte de Ségur, *Mémoires ou Souvenirs et Anecdotes* (ed. F. Barrière, 2 vols, 1879), I, p 68

(c) Anglomania

It would be a wise maxim that every Government should endeavour to preserve its customs and manners as distinct as possible from those of its neighbours and keep alive those patriotic prejudices which are the source of persevering courage in war and a steady attachment to internal produce and manufactures in time of peace, none has so much to reproach itself with an opposite conduct as France, the strong characteristic features that formerly marked the subjects of the monarchy are so much altered, that the French appear to be a different people to what they were before the beginning of the late war [of American Independence]. Different circumstances have concurred to produce this effect, and men of a speculative turn of mind do not fail to discern in it, tho' at a distance, the most important revolutions. The intercourse of the French with the Americans, whose manners and opinions could not but have influence, have brought them nearer to the English than they had ever been before. The almost unrestrained introduction of our daily publications (tolerated indeed by the Government from the conviction of the impossibility of preventing it) have attracted the attention of the people more towards the freedom and advantages of our constitution, has also infused into them a spirit of discussion of public matters which did not exist before. But amongst the most disadvantageous effects of this intercourse, may certainly be reckoned an almost universal taste for the elegancies and luxuries of British manufacture, a taste, which, since the war, has turned the scale of trade entirely against this nation.

> Daniel Hailes to Lord Carmarthen, 25 October 1786, *Despatches from Paris, 1788–1790*, XVI, p 148

(d) National humiliation

The example of the very extraordinary and rapid recovery of Great Britain from the wounds she received in the late War [of American Independence] has not failed to attract the attention of this people;

and the blessings of freedom and justice enjoyed in so eminent a
degree under his Majesty's [George III] paternal reign have excited
85   an ardent desire to attain similar advantages. A sentiment of shame at
the impotence betrayed by France in the late contest in Holland
[1787], and the disgraceful political defeat that followed it, is
strongly and generally impressed on men's minds, and is
accompanied, no doubt, by the conviction that it is vain to attempt
90   to struggle with so vicious a Government against a power that
possess an innate and constitutional superiority.

Despatches from Paris 1788–1790 (ed. Oscar Browning,
Camden Society, Third Series), vol XIX, p 30

Questions

a   What was *haute, moyenne* and *basse justice* (line 14)?
b   What indirect criticisms does Voltaire make of France in writing
about the British constitution?
c   Why did the American envoys seem to bring a 'flavour of
antiquity' into the French kingdom?
★   d   How far did the rise of the United States of America make
democratic ideas acceptable to French opinion in the *ancien
régime*?

II   The Pre-Revolution 1785–89

Introduction

By 1785 there were increasing signs that the political system of the *ancien régime*, which had already been under strain when Louis XVI began his reign, was breaking down. The government could no longer meet its expenses, the economic depression was worsening, the working of the various administrative institutions was being questioned, and various groups of people were making known their growing collection of grievances, resentments and hardships. At the same time the political and social, moral and religious beliefs and principles, which had upheld the regime, were losing their hold. This was the situation in which two successive Controllers-General, Charles Alexandre de Calonne and Loménie de Brienne, struggled in vain to put forward plans for financial reform against opposition from an Assembly of Notables and the Parlement of Paris as representatives of the privileged classes. Their failure led to the summoning of the Estates-General for the first time since 1614, but the success of the *révolte nobiliaire* was threatened by popular resentment at the attitude of the Parlement of Paris towards the composition of the Estates-General:

1 This section begins with the affair of the diamond necklace, from which Napoleon dated the Revolution. This is an exaggeration, but the trivial episode added to the decline in the estimation of the royal family by public opinion. Further extracts contain contemporary views about the dissatisfaction of the times and fears about the decline of religion and royalism.

2 The extracts here are concerned with the unsuccessful attempt of Calonne, who had been Controller-General since 1783, to secure support for his reforms from an Assembly of Notables, an ancient body consisting of bishops, princes, great noblemen, judges and officials, which had last met in 1626, to avoid summoning the Estates-General. Its opposition to him, together with the hostility of Necker's supporters, led to his dismissal in 1787.

3 His successor, Brienne, adopted almost all of Calonne's plans, including his scheme for the creation of provincial assemblies to supervise the collection of the proposed general land tax, and he hoped to induce the parlements to register his edicts. The extracts in this section refer to the opposition to the reforms made by the

parlements and, as regards the proposed toleration for Protestants, by the French Church.

4 Brienne's failure and the worsening financial situation had serious consequences. The king announced the summoning of the Estates-General. Brienne, after virtually declaring national bankruptcy by suspending treasury payments, resigned, and Necker returned to office. Meanwhile, the economic depression, worsened by the bad harvest of 1788, was arousing popular discontent.

5 This section indicates the political situation during the preparation for the Estates-General. The controversy following the insistence by the Parlement of Paris that the Estates-General should meet as it had in 1614 is illustrated here in 1 of some 25 pamphlets which appeared each week for a period of 6 weeks. The Princes of the Blood clearly understood the issues at stake, but the government had to grant the third estate the double representation it wanted. The cahiers or memoranda drawn up by assemblies of electors of the Estates-General represented the wishes of the well-to-do urban middle classes and the better-off farmers. The poorer classes could only express their grievances by rioting such as occurred at Marseilles.

1 The Approaching Storm

(a) The diamond necklace affair, 1785

The central fact in the whole miserable affair was that Mme. de la Motte had the audacity to pretend that the Queen of France had given a rendezvous to the Cardinal de Rohan at night in the gardens of Versailles, had spoken to him, offered him a rose and allowed him
5   to throw himself at her feet, and that the cardinal believed that the queen had done this. That was the crime against religion and against royalty. . . . The revolution already existed in men's minds, when they could treat such an insult to the king, in the person of the queen, with such indifference.

> Mons. Beugnot, avocat, in Alfred Cobban, *Aspects of the French Revolution* (1968), p 88

(b) Its result for the queen

10   The carefree, joyous days were gone, never to return. It was farewell to those tranquil and informal holidays at her beloved Trianon; farewell forever to those brilliant fêtes and galas which served as a showcase for all the glittering splendour, the sparkling wit, the exquisite good taste of French court life. What was more, it was
15   farewell forever to respect and reverence for the institution of monarchy.

> *Mémoires de Marie-Antoinette par Madame Campan* (2 vols, 1823) in Annunziata Asquith, *Marie Antoinette* (1974), p 127

(c) Declining religion

It ought, above all, to be considered that there has grown up, of late years, a spirit of enquiry into the measures of Government, an opposition (if I may call it) of Public Opinion of so forcible a nature, that it has been respected by Ministers even of the most arbitrary Principles. Religion, or rather Superstition of the Church of Rome, for a long time upheld the authority of the Sovereign; but that which may be looked upon to have been in a manner, the Key Stone of the Vast Pile of Absolute Power, is now dropt out, or rather worn away from the Building. Human Reason, which had been fettered and restrained during so many centuries, having at last shaken off the Yoke of Spiritual Tyranny is now, in the natural progress of freedom, proceeding to enquire into its Temporal Rights, and perhaps, to contend for a limitation of those powers of Government under which it has been so long oppressed.

Daniel Hales to Lord Carmarthen, 17 April 1788, *Despatches from Paris 1788—1790*, XIX, pp 30–31

(d) Prevailing discontents

I was surprised, on my being introduced into various Parisian circles in 1786, to hear such unreserved political talk, and that of a nature which I had supposed would infallibly lead to the Bastille. Its prevailing tenour was, that neither the finances nor the authority of the government could long be supported; that the people would not long bear the excessive taxes and excessive oppression under which they groaned; and that the French in general were ardently desirous, and strongly flattered themselves with the hopes of being, in a very few years, governed as we are. This was the conversation of people of consideration and property, even connected with the court, and shining in the elevated walks of life. The prevailing sentiments of most ranks were much in favour of the English, as the wonderful adoption of our tastes and fashions of late years, and the avidity with which our publications were read, abundantly evince.

James Edward Smith, Paris, 1787, J. M. Thompson (ed.), *English Witnesses of the French Revolution* (1938), pp 7–8

(e) An army officer's vain suggestion, 1787

A war, in the critical situation facing royal authority, could only be helpful. Ideas of glory, hope for honourable reward, the habitual disposition of the army to enjoy taking risks, the fortunes of battle, especially the magnanimous protection of a defenceless people, exposed by its very leaders to the arms of the enemy, would have

50   created diversions from internal policies and probably have led the
      troops to make common cause with royal authority.

> Alexandre de Lameth, *Histoire de l'Assemblée constituante
> 1789–90* (2 vols, 1828), I, p lxxviii in Jean Egret, *The French
> Prerevolution 1787–88* (trans. W. D. Camp, 1977), p 42

Questions

a   What was Marie Antoinette's 'beloved Trianon' (line 11)?
b   Why is the French Church called 'the Key Stone of the Vast Pile
    of Absolute Power' in extract *c* (lines 23–4)?
c   Why were even courtiers and wealthy people in France 'much in
    favour of the English' (line 42)?
*   d   Why did France suffer a 'temporary annihilation in the political
    scales of Europe' (Thomas Jefferson) during the latter part of the
    eighteenth century?

2   Calonne and the Notables

(a) The assembly of notables

However difficult it may be to foretell the result of this Meeting, it is
nevertheless obviously the consequence of embarrassment in the
Finances to which the Controller-Général finds himself alone
unequal and which he has not the courage to face. The good effects of
5   this measure are already conspicuous: the paternal goodness of His
Majesty in thus calling together a meeting of His Subjects of
different ranks in order to concert means of general relief and benefit
to the community at large is talk'd of in terms of the highest praise
and satisfaction.
10   The friends and well-wishers of Monsr. de Calonne are warm in
their encomiums upon him, while others less prejudic'd are
persuaded that little real advantage is to be expected, and consider
the measure rather as a proof of a pressing emergency, and that,
unless some at present unforeseen expedient shall be hit upon, some
15   new system of economy for diminishing the civil establishment of
the Royal Family, the arrears of debt must ever continue to be
enormous.

> Lord Dorset to Lord Carmarthen, 4 January 1787, *Despatches
> from Paris*, XVI, p 168

(b) The king's opening of the assembly, 22 February 1787

Gentlemen, I have selected you in the different orders of the State,
and I have assembled you around me to make you part of my
20   purposes.
    This has been the practice of several of my predecessors, and

notably the head of my line, whose name remains dear to all Frenchmen, and whose example I ever glory in following.

The plans which will be revealed to you on my behalf are large and important. On the one hand, to improve the revenues of the State and to free them from all constraint by a fairer imposition of taxation; and on the other, to free trade from the different restrictions which hinder its circulation, and to relieve, as far as circumstances allow me, the poorest part of my subjects: such are, Gentlemen, the projects with which I am occupied and am determined to pursue after the most mature consideration. Because they are all conducive to the public good, and I know the zeal for my service with which you are inspired, I do not hesitate to consult you over their execution; I will hear and consider carefully whatever observations you consider apply to them. I trust that your advice, directed entirely towards the same end, will display ready agreement, and that no private interest will oppose itself to the general good.

Archives parlementaires de 1787 à 1860 . . . Première série 1787–99 (Second Edition, 1879–1914), I, p 196

(c) Calonne's defence of his policy

I shall easily show that it is impossible to tax further, ruinous to be always borrowing and not enough to confine ourselves to measures of economy, and that, with matters as they are, ordinary ways are unable to lead us to our goal, and the only effective remedy, the only means of managing finally to put the finances truly in order, must consist in reviving the entire State by recasting all that is unsound in its constitution. I shall show that the disparity, discord and incoherence of the various parts of the body of the monarchy result from the constitutional defects that sap its strength and impede its functioning; that we cannot eliminate any one of them without attacking them all in the primary factor which caused them originally and still perpetuates them; that this [factor] alone infects everything, harms everything and prevents any improvement; that a kingdom composed of *pays d'état, pays d'élection, administrations provinciales* and *administration mixtes* – a Kingdom whose provinces are foreign one to another; where multiple internal frontiers separate and divide the subjects of the same sovereign; where certain regions are totally freed from taxes, the full weight of which is therefore borne by other regions; where the richest class is the least taxed; where privilege prevents all stability; where neither a constant rule nor a common will is possible – such a state is inevitably a very imperfect kingdom, full of corrupt practices and impossible to govern well. In effect, the result is that general administration is excessively complicated, public contributions unequally spread, trade hindered by countless restrictions, circulation obstructed in all

its branches, agriculture crushed by overwhelming burdens; the
65 state's finances impoverished by excessive costs of recovery and by
variations in their yield. Finally, I shall prove that so many abuses, so
visible to all eyes, and so justly censured, have only until now
resisted a public opinion which condemns them, because no body
had attempted to destroy their roots and eliminate the origin of all
70 obstacles by establishing a more uniform order.

Réponse de M. de Calonne à l'écrit de M. Necker, publié en avril
1787 (1788), pp 50–51

Questions

a   Who was 'the head of my line' (line 22) and what were *pays d'état*,
    pays d'élection, administrations provinciales and *administrations mixtes*
    (lines 52–3)?
b   What social and economic aims were set before the notables in
    extracts *b* and *c*, and what counter-proposal to solve the financial
    crisis is revealed in extract *a*?
c   Compare Calonne's criticism of the 'consitutional defects' of the
    ancien régime in extract *c* and those made previously by Turgot
    (p 18)
★ d   Calonne's failure with the Assembly of Notables 'is characteristic
    of that lack of political sense which he invariably exhibited'
    (Alfred Cobban). Discuss this judgement.

3   Brienne and the Parlement

(a) The Parlement of Paris

The Parlement of Paris has made slow but constantly-pursued
progress towards establishing itself, following the example of the
English parliament, as the representative body of the nation. The
uncertain position of the government invites it to profit from the
5 situation; and what an immense authority the parlement would
acquire if it succeeded in its ambitious designs! Taxes would become
the family inheritance of its members, who would be veritable
hereditary sovereigns, the more powerful through possessing the
advantage of being co-legislators with the monarch; they would
10 have also the formidable right of pronouncing without appeal upon
the property and life of citizens.

Mémoires de Marquis de Ferrières (2 vols, 1821), I, p 10

(b) Another view of the parlement

10 July 1787 Our affairs are more troubled than ever. The edicts of
the King to establish the two taxes needed to refund the deficit
brought about by the extravagant M. de Calonne, which are the
15 stamp-duty and the land-tax in a new form devised by M. de

Toulouse, and most likely to succeed under the administration of the provincial assemblies, have been rejected by the Parlement for registration. They declare that this time they are not a party willing to consent to the taxes, they who for nearly a century have allowed taxation to crush us and permitted M. de Calonne all his extravagences and borrowing of which they have been perfectly aware. They call for the Estates–General, the most vicious and false assembly that any nation has ever had, instead of allowing us to form and establish the provincial governments in which the deputies would have been in future true and perfect representatives, much better than yours, who nevertheless defend your people and their liberty. Finally, my lord, I consider them on this occasion to be veritable enemies of the public good and the re-establishment of order.

> *Lettres de l'Abbé Morellet à Lord Shelburne 1772–1803* (1898), pp 244–5

(c) The edict establishing provincial assemblies, 22 June 1787

I. There shall immediately be established, in all the provinces of our kingdom where there are no provincial Estates, one or more provincial assemblies, in accordance with a decision to be determined by us, and, wherever local circumstances allow, special assemblies for districts and towns, and, during the intervals between the holding of the said assemblies, intermediary commissions, all composed of any of our subjects of the three orders paying land or personal taxes in the said provinces, districts and towns, without nevertheless the number of persons chosen in the first two orders exceeding the number of persons chosen for the third estate, and that the votes shall be counted by heads among the members of the different orders separately.

II. The said provincial assemblies shall be . . . charged . . . with the assessment and collection of all land and personal taxes, both those of which the proceeds must be conveyed to our royal treasury, and those which have or will have been levied for roads, public works, damages, subsidies, repairing of churches and presbyteries and other expenditure whatsoever. . . .

V. It will be legal for the said provincial assemblies to make any representations to us and to inform us of such projects as they shall judge beneficial to our people. . . .

VI. We reserve to ourselves to determine, by particular rules, what concerns the first meeting of the said assemblies, their composition . . . as well as their procedure . . . .

> J. M. Roberts (ed.), *French Revolution Documents 1787–92* (1966), p 8

(d) Opposition by the parlements

The Parliament of Paris, and, indeed, all the other Parliaments of the
Kingdom, continue to be animated by the same spirit of opposition
to the measures of the Court that has manifested itself in so
uncommon a degree ever since the dissolution of the Assembly of
Notables. The protection of the people from an increase of taxes is
the ground . . . that has artfully been chosen by the Parliament on
which to rest their disobedience; but, I have reason to think that the
establishment of the Provincial Assemblies throughout the
Kingdom (a measure which could not be opposed by them in an
open manner, on account of its extreme popularity) is the real, tho'
concealed, motive of their conduct. That innovation, which
however it may be lightly treated with respect to its consequences to
the constitution of the French monarchy by some individuals,
seems, in general, to be allowed to be a change of great prospective in
importance. But, if, as it is imagined, these establishments should in
future conduce to the limitation of the authority of the Sovereign,
there can be no doubt but that they will affect in a more dear and
more immediate manner the consideration of those Courts whose
existence is almost coeval with the monarchy itself. The Provincial
Assemblies becoming hereafter the judges and regulators of every
part of the administration that immediately affects the people, and of
which they are to form so considerable a part, nothing can in future
be effectually opposed by the Parliaments, as their sanction can never
be witheld from such measures as may already have been adopted,
and agreed to by the nation at large.

Daniel Hailes to Lord Carmarthen, 16 August 1787,
Despatches from Paris, XVI, pp 231–2

(e) Toleration for Protestants

The great act of legislation which the king wishes to announce to
you, Gentlemen, to accord civil rights to those of his subjects who
do not profess the Catholic religion, is in accordance with his plans
of government, the development of which you will comprehend, to
the glory of France and the happiness of the people.

In observing the abuses which call for the remedy of the laws, he
has seen that it is necessary, either to banish from his State the
numerous portion of his subjects who do not profess the Catholic
religion, or to assure them a legal status. . . . His Majesty does not
wish there to be any other public worship in his kingdom than that of
the Catholic, Apostolic and Roman religion. This holy religion, in
which the king was born, and beneath which the kingdom has
flourished, will always be the only public and authorized religion in
the State.

His Majesty recognizes the legal rights which mark the births,
marriages and deaths of his non-catholic subjects, and he extends his

justice to them with regard to these age–long observances, which are a sacred natural right rather than an arbitrary concession of the law.

Every enlightened section of the nation has wanted this law for a long time, which His Majesty has only put forward after the most careful consideration.

To the great advantages which will result for the population, for agriculture, for trade and for the arts, will also be joined that of no longer seeing the contradiction between the law and nature, between the laws and the judgements of tribunals, and finally between the supporters of ordinances and the invincible evidence of facts.

The king's non-catholic subjects will be protected by laws which will assure their status without making them dangerous; and the wise tolerance of their religion, being thus restricted to the most incontestable rights of human nature, should not be confused with a blameworthy indifference towards all faiths.

The Speech of the Keeper of the Seals to the Parlement of Paris, 19 November 1787, *Archives parlementaires*, I, pp 267–9

(f) The misgivings of the clergy

The French clergy are far from disputing with the unfortunate remnants of Protestantism over the legal and authentic rites which mark the three great epochs of human life. We do not applaud less sincerely the provisions of the edict, which uphold in favour of non–catholics the free enjoyment of their rights, privileges and possessions, and guarantee them the peaceful exercise of the arts, skills and customary professions. . . . But heresy could one day take advantage of this general statement to remove the line of demarcation placed by the law of the kingdom between Catholics and those who profess a religion different from the religion of the State. It is necessary to distinguish the man from the citizen, civil rights from natural rights: if the latter are independent of religion, the former are often subordinated to it in their exercise, and all political bodies must determine the qualities which it exacts from its members and dependants. One of the principal prerogatives of the citizen is the power to perform the obligations, privileges and duties of society. In France, no one has the right to share in these without professing the national religion. This is the principle of the religious test which always precedes admission to public offices, and even in commissions concerning public order. . . .

Far from us the thought of harming or humiliating the non-catholics: we will always respect their persons, honour their talents and protect their possessions. If we ask with such insistence that they should not be nominated to positions, employments and activities which afford an influence on general affairs, on municipal administration, on the education of the young, on the determination of festivals and on public opinion, it is because the faith of the

kingdom would be endangered, and because the Christian charity,
which we owe to our erring brethren, must be allied with that
evangelical force which must never yield to error.

Rémonstrance du clergé de France au roi sur l'édit de 19 Nov. 1787,
Bayet and Albert, op cit, pp 437–40

Questions

a Why did the parlement want the Estates-General to be
summoned?

b Why was the proposal to establish provincial assemblies opposed
by the parlement, but popular in the kingdom?

c Why did the assurances of the Keeper of the Seals (extract *e*) on
toleration for the Protestants not satisfy the French clergy
(extract *f*)?

★ d Why did the French system of administration break down in the
years before 1789?

4 The Growing Crisis

(a) *The threat of bankruptcy*

Paris, 17 October 1787 – Dined to-day with a party, whose
conversation was entirely political. . . . One opinion pervaded the
whole company, that they are on the eve of some great revolution in
the government; that everything points to it; the confusion in the
5   finances great; with a *déficit* impossible to provide for without the
States-General of the kingdom, yet no ideas formed of what would
be the consequence of their meeting; no minister existing, or to be
looked to in or out of power, with such decisive talents as to promise
any other remedy than palliative ones; a prince on the throne, with
10   excellent dispositions, but without the resources of a mind that could
govern in such a moment without ministers; a court buried in
pleasure and dissipation, and adding to the distress, instead of
endeavouring to be placed in a more independent situation; a great
ferment amongst all ranks of men, who are eager for some change,
15   without knowing what to look for, or to hope for; a strong leaven of
liberty, increasing every hour since the American Revolution;
altogether form a combination of circumstances that promise e'er
long to ferment into motion, if some master hand, of very superior
talents, and inflexible courage, is not found, at the helm to guide
20   events, instead of being driven by them. It is very remarkable that
such conversation never occurs, but a bankruptcy is a topic. . . .

Arthur Young, op cit, pp 84–5

(b) *The summoning of the Estates-General*

His Majesty can announce to his subjects that the assembly of the

Estates-General is fixed for the 1st. May next, and it is with satisfaction that His Majesty envisages the moment when he will find himself surrounded by the generous and faithful representatives of the nation that he has the happiness to govern. Assured of gaining the happy consequences of their zeal and their love, he enjoys in advance the consoling hope of seeing serene and tranquil days succeed these days of storm and anxiety; order everywhere restored; the public debt entirely consolidated; and France enjoying without an increase of burdens the respect assured her by her territory, her wealth and the character of her inhabitants.

Arrêt de Conseil d'Etat, 8 August 1788, *Archives parlementaires*, I, p 387

(c) The suspension of treasury payments

Financial difficulties notwithstanding, great economies, severe retrenchments and the progressive extinction of impositions and life-annuities did promise resources, which successive loans should have provided the time to expect; and, if nothing had troubled the inauguration and performance of operations ordained by His Majesty, public confidence would have been upheld, these loans would have been repaid, the sacrifices which they exacted would have been justified by the selfless virtue of fidelity to all engagements; obligations would have been met with exactitude, and borrowing could even have been reduced.

But, owing to circumstances which His Majesty prefers not to recall, public confidence has been undermined by those very people who should have been ready to uphold it; public loans have been denounced as if they were not necessary and discredited as if their security were uncertain; the badness of the weather, through increasing the need for relief and making debts more difficult to recover, has still further increased the disquiet; undertakings have become more difficult and resources less abundant; and, as nearly always happens in times of general disquiet, the trouble is made worse by the very concern of everyone to save himself.

Amid these difficulties, His Majesty has not despaired of the nation's fortune; he has considered that, if its distress is great, its resources are even greater; that nothing is threatened except by anxiety and fear, and, since the crisis should become less serious as the meeting of the Estates-General approaches, there is need for provisional arrangements which should be followed by a complete recovery.

These arrangements must be such that, until the meeting of the Estates-General and even throughout the year 1789, all payments are assured, and the undertakings most affecting the public credit are safeguarded from all alarm and disquiet. . . .

This is what His Majesty wishes to achieve in ordering that a part

65   of payments made by the royal cashier will be made, not in paper
     money, since His Majesty is aware of its inconvenience and risks, but
     in certificates of the royal treasury, proportionate to these payments
     and intended to satisfy them.
         These certificates of the royal treasury will carry interest at five per
70   cent; and when circumstances allow His Majesty to raise a loan, these
     will be accepted there as readily as legal coinage.
         The Preamble to the Royal Edict, 16 August 1788, ibid,
         pp 354–5

(d) The resulting panic (1)

Paris, 20 August 1788 – The want of money . . . has in fact overborne
all their resources, and the day before yesterday they [the
government] published an arrêt suspending all reimbursements of
75   capital and reducing the payment of the principal mass of demands
for interest to 12 sous in the livre, the remaining eight sous to be paid
with certificates. . . . The consternation is as yet too great to let us
judge of the issue. It will probably open the public mind to the
necessity of a change in their consitution and to the submitting the
80   collected wisdom of the whole in place of a single will, by which
they have hitherto been governed. It is a remarkable proof of the
total incompetency of a single head to govern a nation well, when
with a revenue of six hundred millions they are led to a declared
bankruptcy, and to stop the whole of government, even in its most
85   essential movements, for want of money.
         The Papers of Thomas Jefferson (ed. J. P. Boyd, 21 vols,
         1950–83), XIII, pp 529–30

(e) The resulting panic (2)

The step taken lately by the Ministers in fixing the Convocation of
the States-General for the 1st. of May next, has not produced the
effect that was expected, and . . . that which was made public on
Tuesday last has thrown everybody into the greatest alarm. It would
90   be sufficient to inclose the Arrêt which bears the date 16th. of this
month in order to enable your Lordship to judge of its consequences:
the failure of the engagements of Government they formally
announced, although it may have been expected by many, yet it
seems to have excited nearly as much surprise as consternation. . . .
95   So great was the alarm occasioned by this Arrêt. . . . that the loan of
125 millions which had always been considered favourably by the
Public was done at 30 per cent loss; Annuities were sold at four years
purchase, and the shares of the Caisse d'Escompte fell suddenly 200
Livres per share, and thousands pressed forwards to convert their
100 paper into Money. . . . All these disasters are attributed by the
Court . . . to the Parliments; to their secret practices and their open
opposition to every reasonable measure of Government: they

continue to be treated as ambitious usurpers of the King's Authority acting merely from interested motives, and covering their views of exemption from all contributions to the State, under the pretext of vigilance and care for the public safety:– on the other hand, dispersed though these Bodies are for the most part at present, they do not want for Advocates, and the tide of popular opinion continues to run strongly in their favour.

> Daniel Hales to Lord Carmarthen, 21 August 1788, *Despatches from Paris*, XIX, pp 90–1

(f) Agrarian distress (1)

The high price of Corn has occasioned many insurrections in some of the Provincial Towns, and particularly at Rheims and Vendôme: at St. Quentin a barge laden with 2000 sacks of the above-mentioned commodity belonging to a very rich Individual of that place, who was accused in the neighbouring Villages of having made his fortune by entirely engrossing that Article, was seized upon by the populace, and the whole of the cargo was thrown into the River.

> Lord Dorset to Lord Carmarthen, 19 March 1789, ibid, II, p 175

(g) Agrarian distress (2)

In the early spring of 1789, after the terrible winter which had caused so much suffering amongst the poor, the Duc d'Orléans – Egalité – was very popular in Paris. The previous year he had sold many paintings from the fine collection in his palace, and it was generally believed that the eight millions raised by the sale had been devoted to relieving the sufferings of the people during the hard winter which had just ended. In contrast, whether rightly or wrongly, there was no mention of any charitable gifts from the royal princes or from the king and queen. . . . Nor did the king ever show himself. Hidden away at Versailles or hunting in the nearby forests, he suspected nothing, foresaw nothing and believed nothing he was told.

> *Escape from Terror, The Journal of Madame de la Tour du Pin* (ed. and trans. Felice Harcourt, Folio Society, 1979), p 79

Questions

a Why was the Estates-General summoned?

b What explanations of 'circumstances which His Majesty prefers not to recall' (lines 43–4) are offered by extracts *a*, *d* and *e* in considering the origins of France's financial difficulties?

c What was the nature of the financial (lines 98–100) and commercial (lines 112–16) expedients adopted by some people during this time of crisis?

★ d How did the financial and economic crisis increase social tensions in pre-Revolutionary France?

5   Preliminaries to the Estates-General

(a) The parlement's refusal

After considering the summoning, composition and numbers which
marked the Estates-General of 1614, the court declares:

With regard to the first subject, the court is obliged to revive the
form practised at this time, that is to say the summoning by
5   bailiwicks and seneschelships, not by provinces or generalities; this
form, consecrated from century to century by the most numerous
examples and by the last Estates-General, is above all the only way of
obtaining the complete appearance of the electors by their estates
before independent officers.

10   With regard to the composition, the court has neither power nor
obligation to bring about the slightest diminution of the right of
electors, a right that is natural, constitutional and respected up to the
present, to give power to those citizens whom they judge the most
worthy.

15   As regards numbers, those of the respective deputies, not being
determined by any law nor by any constant usage for any order, it is
in neither the power nor the intention of this court to add to them;
the said court can only in this respect rely upon the wisdom of the
king regarding measures required to achieve such modifications as
20   reason, liberty, justice and the general will may indicate.

Arrêt du Parlement, 5 December 1788, *Archives parlementaires*,
I, p 550

(b) An anti-parlementaire pamphlet

What motives have led the Parlement of Paris to demand the meeting
of the Estates-General under the form of 1614? Is it in virtue of
tradition? There are older forms. Is it to conform to present
circumstances? The facts are to the contrary. . . .

25   In addition, what right has the Parlement of Paris to prescribe the
form of the Estates-General? I: is not empowered to do so by the
nation, and it has itself recognized its inability to do this. Does it wish
to retract, and going back on a statement compelled, it is true, by
necessity, renew its former pretensions? . . .

30   It is either error or bad faith to say that it is from a desire not to
change the constitution, not to make innovations, not to upset the
established order; the real meaning of this assertion is a wish not to
change the actual situation, that is not to reform the prevailing
abuses; and, if one notices who expresses the fears, one will always
35   find that it is those people who benefit from these very abuses.

But if we have a constitution, which is a settled form of
government accepted or endured by our forefathers, does it follow
that we are bound to preserve and accept it? Certainly not, because it
is a national right of all nations, and still more a national right of

mankind, that no one can bind another, and it is both unjust and
absurd that the dead can constrain the living and that one generation
imposes an obligation upon another.

J. M. Roberts (ed.), op cit, p 50

(c) A protest by the princes of the blood

Derived from the new theories, from the determination to change
rights and laws, is the claim put forward by several sections of
the third estate that their order should obtain two votes in the
Estates-General while each of the two leading orders continue to have
only one.

The undersigned princes will not repeat what has been expressed
by several committees [of the Notables], namely the injustice and
danger of innovations in the composition of the Estates-General or
in the form of summoning it; the large number of claims which
would result from this; the ease, if votes were counted by heads and
without distinction of orders, of compromising, by the corruption
of a few members of the third estate, the interests of this order,
which are well protected in the present constitution; the destruction
of the equilibrium, which has been so wisely established between the
three orders, and of their independence.

It has been demonstrated to Your Majesty how important it is to
preserve the only form of summoning the Estates-General that is
constitutional, the form hallowed by law and custom, the distinction
between the orders, the right to deliberate in separate chambers, the
equality of votes [between them], which are the unalterable
foundations of the French monarchy.

The Memorandum of the Princes of the Blood, 12 December
1788, *Archives parlementaires*, I, p 488

(d) The Council's decision

The King, having heard the report delivered in his Council by the
Minister of his Finances concerning the forthcoming summoning of
the Estates-General, has adopted its principles and ordains as
follows:

1. That the deputies to the forthcoming Estates-General will
number at least a thousand.

2. That this number will be decided, as far as possible, in
accordance with the population of each bailiwick and the taxation
paid by it.

3. That the number of deputies for the third estate shall equal that
of the two other orders together and that this proportion will be
established by the letters of convocation.

4. That these preliminary decisions shall provide the basis for the
work required to draw up immediately the letters of convocation
and other related documents.

5. That the report delivered to His Majesty will be printed after
80 the present decision.

Résultat du Conseil, 27 December 1788, ibid., I, p 496

(e) A summary of the cahiers

The Committee of Constitution in the National Assembly, 27 July 1789.

RESULT OF THE ABSTRACT OF THE CAHIERS
ACCEPTED PRINCIPLES
85   1. The French govenment is a monarchical government.
      2. The person of the King is inviolable and sacred.
      3. His crown is hereditary from male to male.
      4. The King is the depository of executive power.
      5. Those who exercise its authority are responsible.
90   6. Royal sanction is necessary for the promulgation of laws.
      7. The nation makes law with royal sanction.
      8. National consent is necessary for borrowing and taxation.
      9. Taxation can only be agreed from one session of the Estates-
         General to the other.
95   10. Property is sacred.
     11. Individual liberty is sacred.

QUESTIONS ON WHICH THE CAHIERS ARE NOT
UNIVERSALLY AGREED
      1. Has the King legislative power limited by the constitutional
100   laws of the kingdom?
      2. Can the King alone make personal laws concerning police and
         administration in the intervals between the sessions of the
         Estates-General?
      3. Shall these laws be submitted to the free registration of the
105   Sovereign Courts?
      4. Can the Estates-General only be dissolved by itself?
      5. Can the King alone summon, prorogue and dissolve the
         Estates-General?
      6. Is the King obliged after a dissolution to issue another summons
110   at once?
      7. Should the Estates-General be permanent or periodic?
      8. If periodic, should there not be an intermediary Commission?
      9. Should the first two orders be united into a single Chamber?
     10. Should the two Chambers be composed without distinction of
115   order?
     11. Should the members of the order of the Clergy be included
         among the two other orders?
     12. Should the representatives of the Clergy, the Nobility and the
         Commons be in the proportion of one, two or three?

13. Should a third Order be established under the title of the Order of the Countryside?
14. Should persons possessing pensions, employment or places at the Court be deputies of the Estates-General?
15. Are two-thirds of the votes necessary to pass a resolution?
16. Should taxes having the object of liquidating the national debt be continued until it is entirely extinguished?
17. Should *lettres de cachet* be abolished or restricted?
18. Should the freedom of the press be complete or restricted?

L. G. Wickham Legg (ed.), *Select Documents of the French Revolution* (2 vols, 1905), I, pp 103–4

(f) Revolt at the elections

The fermentation which has manifested itself lately in different parts of this Kingdom has been carried to a very serious and alarming length, particularly at Marseilles, where the most daring and, it may be added, cruel outrages have been committed. Amongst the various accounts that are given of this affair, the following I have reason to think comes nearest to the truth. On the day appointed for the Meeting of the Nobility for the Election of Deputies to the States-General the populace assembled under the pretext of the distress they were suffering on account of the dearness of bread, and surrounded the Assembly-House in a very tumultuous manner; their violence increasing and every effort to appease proving ineffectual, the Meeting was broken up, and the Members retired to their several homes in the most private manner possible: this served but to increase the tumult, for the populace then proceeded to pillage the houses of those of the Nobility who were most obnoxious to them; amongst others that of the Bishop of Toulon was a marked object of their fury: the Bishop found means to escape in disguise out of the Town, and, as soon as his flight was discovered, the mob, after destroying all the furniture, etc., threw his carriage and horses into the sea; a Gentleman of the place (some accounts say the Mayor, and that he drew upon himself the rage of the Populace by firing at and killing one of them upon the spot) fell a Victim and was butchered in a manner too shocking to be related with all the circumstances of savage cruelty that were exercised upon his body. The Comte de Caraman assembled the Troops, but they were soon overpowered by Numbers, for the populace were provided with Arms, and he, seeing no other chance of restraining the fury of the moment, had recourse to the Comte of Mirabeau for his influence with the people, and his interference succeeded so far as to obtain a temporary cessation of the outrages.

Lord Dorset to the Duke of Leeds, 9 April 1789, *Despatches from Paris*, XIX, p 184

Questions

a What did the Princes of the Blood consider were the implications of the proposals to change the Estates-General?

b How far were the cahiers agreed in wanting a parliamentary monarchy on British lines in France?

c Accounts for Mirabeau's 'influence with the people' (line 156).

★ d 'The Parlement's popularity vanished overnight' (John Hardman). Why did it lose the support of the third estate in the autumn of 1788?

III The Estates-General May–June 1789

Introduction

The representatives of the third estate came to Versailles eager to obtain the reforms they desired. Since they had secured double representation in the Estates-General and were supported by the parish clergy, they had a good majority over the bishops and noblemen who were opposed to them. The government, however, failed to produce a royal programme of reform for consideration and insisted on retaining the old procedure by which the three orders debated and voted separately instead of uniting as the third estate wanted to happen. They decided to secure this change by deliberate inaction, and no business was transacted, therefore, by the Estates-General for over two months until the issue was decided. The third estate resolved to call itself the National Assembly and invited the other orders to join it, and finally the King had to order this to take place. This recognition of the new single body, which was now to be known fully as the National Constituent Assembly, was a development which implicitly recognised the political superiority of the third estate that Sieyès had asserted:

1 The beginning of this episode is the subject of this first section of the chapter. The extracts show the Keeper of the Seals, speaking with royal authority at the opening session of the Estates-General, refusing to change the voting procedure and merely urging the privileged orders to relinquish their exemptions from taxation; Louis XVI's easy-going, indecisive nature; the leadership of the Comte de Mirabeau; and the reaction in the country and the court to the situation. These were circumstances which inevitably encouraged mutual suspicion and hostility.

2 Subsequent events led to the establishment of the National Assembly. The third estate adopted this title by a decree, which implied its assumption of national sovereignty and right to change the constitution, and then went on to swear the famous tennis-court oath. The response of the royal ministers was to summon a royal session of the Estates-General (which was to be the last time it met). At this the king was made to announce an extensive programme of reform, but tax-exemptions would only be abolished with the approval of the privileged orders, and the three orders were

instructed to resume meetings in their respective chambers. Events had now, however, made a counter-revolution impossible. A majority of the clergy and some of the nobility had joined the third estate, and there was a rumour that a mob was about to march from Paris upon Versailles. The king ordered the privileged orders to join the third estate, and they reluctantly obeyed him, though their attendance was to last only a short time.

3 These events in the early summer of 1789 took place when the produce of the previous year's bad harvest was exhausted, and the new harvest had not yet been gathered. The extracts here show the widespread, though not universal, shortage of grain in the kingdom and the failure of efforts to relieve it. Such a lack of food, taking place at a time of political uncertainty and excitement, was to add a new, unexpected and violent force to the progress of the Revolution.

1 The Opening of the Estates-General

(a) The first meeting, 5 May 1789

An almost general cry has been heard asking for a double representation in favour of the most numerous of the three orders upon whom falls mainly the burden of taxation.

5   In deferring to this demand, his majesty, Gentlemen, has not changed the traditional manner of voting; and although counting by heads, because it results in a single decision, appears to have the advantage of making the general will more clearly known, the king does not wish this new method to be put into effect unless freely approved by the Estates-General and with his majesty's consent.

10   But whatever may be the decision taken upon this question, whatever may be the relative importance attached to the several matters which must be the subjects of discussion, it cannot be doubted that the most perfect accord should unite the three orders in regard to taxation.

15   Since taxation is an obligation common to all citizens, a sort of tribute and the price of the advantages which society bestows upon them, it is right that the nobility and the clergy should share this burden.

       If the continual and respected privileges of the first two orders of
20   the State have for some time been contrary to the common law, their exemptions have for at least as long appeared more transparent than justified.

The Speech of the Keeper of the Seals, P. J. B. Buchez & P. C. Roux, *Histoire parlementaire de la Révolution française* (4 vols, 1834–8), I, pp 2–3

(b) The king's attitude

We [the Queen's friends] never ceased repeating to the King that the third estate would wreck everything – and we were right. We begged him to restrain then, to impose his sovereignty on party intrigue. The King replied: 'But it is not clear that the third estate are wrong. Different forms have been observed each time the Estates have been held. So why reject verification in common? I am for it.'

The King, it has to be admitted, was then numbered among the revolutionaries – a strange fatality which can only be explained by recognizing the hand of Providence. Meanwhile Paris was unquiet and Versailles scarcely less so. . . .

The King, deceived on the one hand by the Genevan [Necker] . . . paid no attention to the Queen's fears.

This well-informed princess knew all about the plots that were being woven; she repeated them to the King, who replied, 'Look, when all is said and done, are not the third estate also my children – and a more numerous progeny? And even when the nobility lose a proportion of their privileges and the clergy a few scraps of their income, will I be any less their king?'

This false perspective accomplished the general ruin.

> Comtesse d'Adhémar, *Souvenirs sur Marie-Antoinette, archiduchesse d'Autriche, reine de France, et sur la cour de Versailles* (4 vols, 1836), III, pp 156–7, John Hardman, *The French Revolution* (1981), pp 90–1

(c) Mirabeau's caution

Let us hope that the nation's representatives will for the future have a better sense of the dignity of their functions, of their mission, of their character; that they will no longer give way to unbounded enthusiasm at any price and under any circumstances; that, finally, instead of presenting Europe with a picture of themselves as schoolboys who have escaped the rod and are drunk with joy because they have been promised an extra holiday each week, instead of this, show themselves to be men, and to be men of distinction in a nation, which, to be the world's leader, needs only a constitution.

> Comte de Mirabeau, *Les Etats-généraux*, No II, 5 May 1789, pp 19–20, J. Gilchrist and W. J. Murray, *The Press in the French Revolution* (1971), p 47

(d) A standstill in the proceedings

It is scarcely possible to give your Grace an adequate idea of the confusion that prevails at present at Versailles owing to the discussions, hitherto fruitlessly carried on by the several Orders with little if any progress . . . towards an agreement upon a regular form of proceeding.

The Tiers-Etat seem to conduct themselves with a determined firmness, and not at all disposed to give way to the Nobility on any point, while on the other hand the Nobility cannot brook the idea of being dictated to by those whom they have been used to consider
60   their inferiors in point of birth and consideration: the Clergy have evidently shown a desire to conciliate matters, the nature of their Order forming two interests which on this occasion are incompatible, but the extreme inveteracy of the two other Orders against each other has not admitted of any good effect from their
65   efforts.

In the mean time the public is dissatisfied and becoming very impatient of delay occasioned by the disunion of the orders at a time when the Nation had flattered itself that some salutary measures would have been adopted for its relief: under these circumstances too
70   the government is placed in a very awkward predicament. . . .

     Lord Dorset to the Duke of Leeds, 28 May 1789, *Despatches from Paris*, XIX, p 202

(e) *Popular discontent*

9 June 1789 – The business going forward at present in the pamphlet shops of Paris is incredible. . . . This spirit of reading political tracts, they say, spreads into the provinces so that all the presses of France are equally employed. Nineteen-twentieths of these
75   productions are in favour of liberty, and commonly violent against the clergy and nobility; I have to-day bespoke many of this description that have reputation; but inquiring for such as had appeared on the other side of the question, to my astonishment I find there are but two or three that have merit enough to be known. Is it
80   not wonderful, that while the press teems with the most levelling or even seditious principles, that if put into execution would over-turn the monarchy, nothing in reply appears, and not the least step is taken by the court to restrain this extreme licentiousness of publication? It is easy to conceive the spirit that must thus be raised
85   among the people. But the coffee-houses in the Palais Royal present yet more singular and astonishing spectacles; they are not only crowded within, but other expectant crowds are at the doors and windows, listening *à gorge deployé* to certain orators, who from chairs or tables harangue each his little audience: the eagerness with
90   which they are heard, and the thunder of applause they receive for every sentiment of more than common hardiness or violence against the present government, can easily be imagined. I am all amazement at the ministry permitting such nests and hot-beds of sedition and revolt which disseminate among the people every hour principles
95   that by and by must be opposed with vigour, and therefore it seems little short of madness to allow the propagation at present.

     Arthur Young, *Travels in France*, pp 134–5

(f) The deputies and the monarchy

The general enthusiasm which prevailed during the early sessions of the Assembly, the discussion among the deputies of the third estate and nobility, and even of the clergy, filled their Majesties and those attached to the cause of monarchy with increasing alarm. . . . The deputies of the third estate arrived at Versailles with the deepest prejudices against the court. The wicked sayings of Paris never fail to spread throughout the provinces. The deputies believed that the king indulged in the pleasures of the table to a shameful excess. They were persuaded that the queen exhausted the treasury of the state to gratify the most unreasonable luxury.

> *Mémoires de Marie-Antoinette par Madame de Campan* (2 vols, 1823), II, p 37

Questions

a What was the Palais Royal mentioned in extract *e* (line 85)?
b Why did the clergy and nobility not possess the same unity as the third estate?
c What was the result of the failure of the king and his ministers to give a clear lead to the Estates-General?
d Was the hope of peaceful reform destroyed during the first days of the Estates-General?

2 The Creation of the National Assembly

(a) The challenge of the third estate

The Tiers-Etat, finding that there remained no longer any hopes of conciliation between their Order and that of the Nobility, resolved the latter end of last week upon proceeding in a regular way to verify the returns of its Deputies which was accordingly done and the whole completed on Monday last: in consequence of an invitation to the two first Orders on the part of the Tiers-Etat to assemble in common with them, a few of the lower Clergy appeared amongst them, but have since retired to their own Order. On Tuesday the Tiers-Etat passed a vote constituting them the Representatives of the Nation; in the course of the debate upon this occasion very violent language was held against the Clergy and the Nobility, and the Strangers who were present testified their approbation to such a degree, that those members who were known to be desirous of moderating the animosity that prevailed found it expedient to remove from their places to avoid the insults which seemed to threaten them. . . .

The Assembly resolved that the Representatives of the Nation do take upon themselves the public debt, and accordingly voted a Loan of at least 80 millions to answer the present exigencies of the State,

20 directing at the same time that any attempt to collect Taxes without
their authority should be resisted; they declared that in case the
present Assembly should be dissolved, the people would be justified
in refusing to pay any Taxes whatever till such time as that Assembly
should be again convoked in a regular and constitutional manner.
25 One of the Members expressed an earnest wish that something
might be done immediately to relieve the necessities of the poor.

Such I understand to be the substance of what passed yesterday
(the 17th). Matters are every day growing exceedingly critical yet the
King's Authority is still paramount, but if His Majesty once gives
30 His decided approbation of the proceedings, such as they have
hitherto been, of the Tiers-Etat, it will be little short of laying His
crown at their feet.

> Lord Dorset to the Duke of Leeds, 18 June 1789, *Despatches
> from Paris*, XIX, p 215

(b) The assembly's assertion

The title of the National Assembly alone describes accurately the
assembly as it is, not only because the members who compose it are
35 the sole representatives legitimately and publicly known and
verified, but also because they are directly returned by almost the
whole of the nation, and finally because the representation is one and
indivisible, none of the deputies, in whatever order or class they
were elected, has the right to exercise his functions separately from
40 the present assembly.

The assembly will never abandon the hope of uniting in its bosom
all the deputies who are absent to-day; it will not cease to call upon
them to fulfil the obligation imposed upon them to take part in the
holding of the Estates-General. At whatever moment the absent
45 deputies present themselves in the course of this session about to be
opened, it declares in advance that it will hasten to receive them and
to share with them, after the verification of their powers, in
undertaking the great tasks needed to bring about the revival of
France.

> Rédaction de l'Assemblée Nationale, Séance du 17 Juin 1789,
> *Moniteur*, I, pp 82–3, J. M. Roberts, *French Revolution
> Documents*, p 107.

(c) The tennis-court oath, 20 June 1789

50 The National Assembly, considering that, since it has been called
to settle the constitution of the kingdom, to bring about the
regeneration of public order and uphold the true principles of the
monarchy, nothing can prevent it from continuing its deliberations
in whatever place it may be forced to establish itself; and considering
55 also that wherever its members are brought together, there is the
National Assembly.

Decrees that all the members of this assembly shall immediately take solemn oath never to separate, but to assemble wherever circumstances shall demand, until the constitution of the kingdom is established and fixed upon solid foundations, and that the said oath being taken, all the members and each in particular shall by his signature confirm this unshakeable resolution.

> Faustin-Adolphe Hélie, *Les Constitutions de la France* (1880), p 22, H. Butterfield, *Select Documents of European History* (1931), p 67

(d) The king's reply

The king wishes the ancient distinction between the three orders of the State to be preserved in its entirety as being essentially linked to the constitution of his kingdom; and that the deputies freely elected by each of the three orders, forming three chambers, deliberating by order, and able, with the sovereign's assent, to agree to deliberate together, can alone be considered as forming the body of the representatives of the nation. Consequently, the king has declared null and void the decisions taken by the deputies of the order of the third estate on the 17th. of this month, as also any that may be adopted subsequently, as being illegal and unconstitutional.

> *Déclaration du roi, concernant la présente tenue des Etats-Généraux*, 23 June 1789, Buchez and Roux, op cit, II, p 14

(e) The king yields

Entirely occupied in upholding the general well-being of my kingdom and desiring above all that the assembly of the Estates-General should occupy itself with matters concerning the whole nation, after the voluntary acceptance that your order has given to my declaration of the 23rd. of this month, I desire my faithful nobility to unite without delay with the two other orders to hasten the accomplishment of my paternal intentions. . . . This would be a new mark of attachment which my nobility will give me.

> The King to the President of the Nobility, 27 June 1789, *Recueil de documents relatif aux séances des Etats-Généraux* (ed. G. Lefebvre, 5 vols, 1953–62), I (11), p 311

(f) The nobility yields

Your Grace may easily imagine what was really the cause, that nothing but the pressing urgency of the moment could have induced the Nobility to relinquish at once all further design of persevering in their original determination; but when it was seen that the King's personal safety was actually endangered, that was a motive for giving way which could not be resisted; the fermentation of the people, from the moment when the Tiers-Etat had so far gained their

point as to bring over to their Body a part of the other two Orders, for the purpose of verifying their returns in common, became very
90 alarming, added to which some of the Military joined in the popular cry, and the French Guards had even been wrought upon to bind themselves by oath not to support the King under the present circumstances: many of these paraded the capital in small bodies, openly boasting of the engagement they had entered in not to obey
95 their Officers: it may well be conceived the effect this had upon the populace who now became quite ungovernable at Versailles, as well as at Paris, insomuch that the King and the Royal Family were no longer secure from outrage even in the Palace.

Lord Dorset to the Duke of Leeds, 28 June 1789, *Despatches from Paris*, XIV, pp. 225–6

Questions

a What is the meaning of the reference to 'verification' in lines 3 and 36?
b Why did the third–estate want the three orders to sit together?
c What led Louis XVI to give way to the third estate?
★ *d* Why did the union of orders not bring about political stability in France?

3 Worsening Agrarian Distress

(a) The price of bread (1)

10 June 1789 – Everything conspires to render the present period in France critical; the want of bread is terrible; accounts arrive every moment from the provinces of riots and disturbances, and calling in the military, to preserve the peace of the markets. The prices
5 reported are the same as I found at Abbeville and Amiens; 5 *sous* (2½d.) a pound for white bread, and 3½ *sous* to 4 *sous* for the common sort eaten by the poor; these rates are beyond their faculties, and occasion great misery. At Meudon, the police, that is to say the Intendant, ordered that no wheat should be sold on the
10 market without the person taking at the same time an equal quantity of barley. What a stupid and ridiculous regulation, to lay obstacles on the supply, in order to be better supplied; and to show the people the fears and apprehensions of Government, creating thereby an alarm, and raising the price at the very moment they wish to sink it. I
15 have had some conversation on this topic with well-informed persons, who have assured me that the price is, as usual, much higher than the proportion of the crop demanded, and there would have been no real scarcity if Mr. Necker would have left the corn-trade alone; but his edicts of restriction, which have been more comments
20 on his book on the legislation of corn [*Sur la Législation et le Commerce*

des Grains, 1775], have operated more to raise the price than all other causes together.

Arthur Young, op cit, p 135

(b) The price of bread (2)

30 June 1789 – By order of the magistrates no person is allowed to buy more than two bushels of wheat at a market, to prevent monopolizing. It is clear to common sense, that all such regulations have a direct tendency to increase the evil, but it is in vain to reason with people whose ideas are immovably fixed. Being here on a market-day [at Nangis, south-east of Paris], I attended and saw the wheat sold out under this regulation, with a party of dragoons drawn up before the market-cross to prevent violence. The people quarrel with the bakers, asserting the prices they demand for bread are beyond the proportion of wheat, and proceeding from words to scuffling, raise riot, and then run away with bread and wheat for nothing. This has happened at Nangis and many other markets; the consequence was, that neither farmers nor bakers would supply them till they were in danger of starving, and, when they did come, prices under such circumstances must necessarily rise enormously, which aggravated the mischief, till troops became really necessary to give security to those who supplied the markets.

Ibid, p 166

(c) A different experience

The most striking character of the country [of northern France] through which we passed yesterday is its astounding fertility. We went through an extent of seventy miles, and I will venture to say that there is not a single acre, but what was in a state of the highest cultivation. The crops are great beyond any conception I could have had of them – thousands and ten thousands of acres of wheat superior to any that can be produced in England; oats extraordinarily large.

Edward Rigby, *Letters from France in 1789* (ed. Lady Eastlake, 1880), p 10

Questions

a How did Necker's concern for the consumer rather than the cultivator of corn aggravate the situation?

b Why was the shortage of food felt most keenly in and around Paris?

c How extensive was the failure of the harvest of 1788–9 in France?

d To what extent was the French agrarian crisis due to the inability of a primitive system of farming to provide adequately for a growing population?

IV   The Rising of the Masses July–October 1789

Introduction

The recognition of the National Assembly did not bring peace to the political scene. Agrarian distress continued to stimulate popular discontent, and there was fear of a royalist move against the capital and forcible suppression of the National Assembly. The fall of the Bastille and the Grande Peur brought fresh influences and pressures upon the National Assembly. The moderate constitutional and social reform envisaged by its leaders, when opposing the system of the *ancien régime*, had now to go further than they had planned. The National Assembly turned to decreeing the abolition of feudalism and considering the Rights of Man. Another intervention by the Paris mob, however, culminated in the taking of the king and royal family to Paris, where they were soon joined by the Assembly. Those 'October Days' ended the first period of revolutionary violence. The third estate had achieved the defeat of both the royal administration and the nobility, but at the price of placating the popular forces:

1 The tense situation in Paris, which was unsuspected by the court, worsened. Troop movements and the dismissal of Necker, who had been advising concessions to the third estate, was followed by the storming of the Bastille. This resulted in Necker's return to office (for slightly over a year) and the elimination of royal authority in Paris as shown in the last extract of this section. The king now no longer controlled the capital and could not hope to regain it even with his mercenary troops.

2 The fall of the Bastille also stimulated a rising among the peasantry, whose circumstances were described by Arthur Young in the first extract here. Violence erupted in the countryside. Mobs broke down enclosures, occupied common land, killed game and destroyed archives and registers. This culminated in the Grande Peur, originating in rumours that brigands, hired by noblemen, were coming to 'restore order' in the countryside, which brought further peasant attacks on castles and mansions. When it was over, the peasantry was in control in many parts of the provinces, but the violence had threatened property and order throughout France.

3 The solution to this problem adopted by the Assembly was to grant the peasants what they wanted. This was supported by the

group of radical revolutionaries called the Jacobins, but it was disliked by the many landlords in the Assembly. It was decided to retain the money dues, but as the peasants refused to pay them, all feudal rights eventually had to be abolished in July 1792. The legislation of 4 August, however, was seen by revolutionaries as the destruction of hated feudal inequality and by noblemen, including the idealists among them (see p 61), as accomplishing their ruin.

4 Paris feared that the Revolution was not yet safe. A royalist demonstration by regimental officers at Versailles on 1 October led to the 'Bread March of the Women' from Paris to Versailles, which resulted in the return to the capital of both king and government for the first time since Louis XIV's reign. Paris was now in control of the Revolution. And by now a growing number of the nobility became émigrés, taking flight to foreign countries where they hoped to gain military help to regain their position.

1 The Storming of the Bastille

(a) The concentration of troops

The . . . intelligence that the court was drawing troops to Versailles and that several regiments were already on the march soon gave rise to a fresh alarm. Most of the ministers of state, and I was one of them, were kept in ignorance of these orders till their effects became matters of public notoriety. The minister at the head of the War Department spoke of the transaction as a measure of caution rendered necessary by the seditious movements that had recently taken place in Versailles and Paris. This seemingly natural explanation, however, became suspected as soon as it was known that Maréchal Broglio [the military commander at Versailles] had received orders to come to court. For my own part, I was never made perfectly acquainted with the plans that were in agitation; the whole was a system of secrets within secrets, and I believe the King himself was unacquainted with the final view of his advisers, who probably intended to reveal them only by degrees and according to the pressure of circumstances.

> Jacques Necker, *On the French Revolution* (2 vols, 1797), I, pp 213–14

(b) A request to the king

That a very humble address be made to the King, to make known to His Majesty the grave concern felt by the National Assembly of his kingdom at the abuse tolerated for some time in the name of a good King in allowing the approach to the capital and to this town of Versailles a train of artillery and numerous corps of troops, both foreign and French, of which some are already stationed in neighbouring villages, while the formation of several camps on the outskirts of these two towns has been announced.

25   That it represented to the King, not only how much these measures are opposed to the kindly intentions of His Majesty for the relief of his people in this unhappy station of dearness and shortage of corn, but also how much they are contrary to the liberty and honour of the National Assembly and likely to deprive the King and his

30 people of that mutual confidence, which is the monarch's glory and safety, which alone can assure the peace and quiet of the kingdom and finally bring to the nation the inestimable fruits which it expects from the labours and zeal of this Assembly.

    That His Majesty be requested very respectfully to reassure his

35 faithful subjects by giving the necessary orders for the immediate cancelling of these orders, which are equally useless, dangerous and alarming, and for the prompt return of the troops and the train of artillery to the places from where they have been withdrawn.

        Comte de Mirabeau to the National Assembly, 8 July 1789, H. M. Stephens (ed.), *Orators of the French Revolution* (2 vols, 1892), I, pp 90–1

(c) Necker's dismissal and Parisian violence

I despatch a messenger extraordinary to Your Grace to acquaint you

40 with the removal of M. Necker from His Majesty's Councils: this event took place yesterday, and M. Necker left Versailles very privately about 8 o'clock the same evening, intending, it is said, to go to Geneva. . . .

    Last night the mob burnt one of the Gates at the entrance of the

45 Town [Paris] by the Rue de Clichy, having taken offence at the Custom House Officers under some trifling pretext: some Dragoons were ordered to attend, but the mischief was done before they arrived, and nothing further was attempted. Almost every day has produced some act of violence: two men, who had been confined for

50 disorderly behaviour at the works of Montmartre, were released by force the next morning; and a few days ago a man fell a victim to the fury of the populace at the Palais Royal.

        Lord Dorset to the Duke of Leeds, 12 July 1789, *Despatches from Paris*, XIX, p 229

(d) False security

I tell you this little detail to show that we had not the slightest inkling of what was to happen in Paris the next day [14 July]. All we had

55 heard was that there had been a few isolated disturbances at the doors of certain bakers accused by the people of adulterating the flour. . . . When you think that I was so placed [as a Lady-in-Waiting to the Queen] as to hear all that went on . . ., that I went every day to Versailles for supper with Madame de Poix, whose husband was the

Captain of the Guard and a member of the Assembly and saw the King every evening at his 'Coucher' or at Orders, what I am about to tell you is amazing.

So secure did we feel in our safety that at midday, and even later, on 14 July neither my aunt nor I had any idea that there had been the slightest disturbance in Paris.

> *Escape from Terror, The Journal of Madame la Tour du Pin,* pp 87–8

(e) The fall of the Bastille

14 July 1789 – We ran to the end of the Rue St. Honoré. We here soon perceived an immense crowd proceeding towards the Palais Royal with acceleration of an extraordinary kind, but which sufficiently indicated a joyful event, and, as it approached, we saw a flag, some large keys, and a paper elevated on a pole above the crowd, on which was inscribed '*La Bastille est prise and les portes sont ouvertes.*' The intelligence of this extraordinary event, thus communicated, produced an impression upon the crown really indescribable. A sudden burst of the most frantic joy instantaneously took place; every possible mode, in which the most rapturous feelings of joy could be expressed, were everywhere exhibited. Shouts and shrieks, leaping and embracing, laughter and tears, every sound and every gesture, including even what approached to nervous and hysterical affection, manifested, among the promiscuous crowd, such an instantaneous and unanimous emotion of extreme gladness as I should suppose was never before experienced by human beings.

> Edward Rigby, op cit, p 27

(f) The consequences in Paris

Necker [after returning from exile] appeared before the National Assembly and received an innovation. Next, he wanted to go to Paris to enjoy a triumph and show himself at the Hôtel de Ville. As the capital fell within the jurisdiction of my ministerial department [for the *Maison du Roi* and for Paris], I thought the occasion would be propitious to accompany him in order to take possession of the municipal administration of the said city. This was a false step, but Necker readily accepted my offer. We left in his carriage, escorted by the National Guard of Versailles. . . . Finally we reached the Hôtel de Ville. Upstairs we found a table at the head of which were two arm-chairs which I thought had been put there for Necker and myself, both of us being *ministres d'Etat*. The Mayor, Bailly, offered one to Necker and, without ceremony, took the other, indicating to me the first place on the benches along the table where the new town councillors, who had been elected without the King's participation, were sitting. I had, for the sake of peace, to suffer this insolence on the part of the Mayor, hitherto my subordinate (with the title of

Prévot des marchands), who took his orders direct from the Minister
100 for Paris. But royal authority in the capital had already vanished.
      Mémoires de Saint-Priest, ed. Baron de Barante (2 vols, 1929),
      I, pp 240–1 in J. Hardman (ed.), *The French Revolution*,
      pp 105–6

Questions

a What reason was there for the third estate to feel itself threatened
    in the second week of July?
b Why should there have been attacks on customs posts and bakers'
    shops in Paris (lines 44–6 and 54–6)?
c Why was Necker accorded the reception described in extract *f*?
★ *d* Why was the Bastille stormed and what was the symbolic
    importance of this event?

2 The Grande Peur

(a) *A peasant woman's distress*

12 July 1789 – Walking up a long hill, to ease my mare, I was joined
by a poor woman, who complained of the times, and that it was a sad
country. Demanding her reasons, she said her husband had but a
morsel of land, one cow and a poor little horse, yet they had a *franchar*
5 (42 lb.) of wheat and three chickens to pay as a quit-rent to one
seigneur; and four *franchar* of oats, one chicken and one sou to pay to
another, besides very heavy tailles and other taxes. She had seven
children, and the cow's milk helped to make the soup. . . . It was
said, at present, that *something was to be done by some great folks, but she*
10 *did not know who or how*, but God send us better, *car les tailles et les*
droits nous écrasent.
      Arthur Young, op cit, p 173

(b) *A nobleman's complaint*

On 29 July 1789, a party of unknown brigands, together with my
vassals and those of Vrigni, a neighbouring parish to mine, came, to
the number of two hundred, to my castle of Sassy, in the parish of
15 Saint-Christophe, near to Argentan, and, after breaking the locks of
the Closets which held my title-deeds, they took from them a large
collection with the registers which are essential for me, and took
them away or burnt them in the woods near my castle; my guard
could not make any resistance, since he is the only guardian in this
20 estate where I do not reside. These wretches rang the alarm-bell in
the neighbouring parishes to gather to them a greater number. I am
indeed most unfortunate in this loss because I have never imposed
upon my vassals the hateful burdens of traditional feudalism, from
which I am very ready they should be freed in the present

circumstances; but who can ever assess and prove the damage that they have done to my property? I appeal to your wisdom that some means may be devised by the National Assembly to compensate me for what I have lost, resting upon common custom, applicable both to my parishioners and to my property, the title-deeds of which they have burnt.

Comte de Germiny to the National Assembly, 20 August 1789 in Ph. Sagnac and P. Caron, *Les comités de droits féodaux et de législation et l'abolition du régime seigneurial, 1789–93* (1907), p 158

(c) A violent scene

21 July 1789 – I have been witness to a scene curious to a foreigner; but dreadful to Frenchmen that are considerate. Passing through the square of the Hôtel de Ville [in Strasburg], the mob were breaking the windows with stones, notwithstanding an officer and a detachment of horse was in the square. Perceiving that their numbers not only increased, but that they grew bolder and bolder every moment, I thought it worth staying to see what it would end in, and clambered on to the roof of low stalls opposite the building against which their malice was directed. Here I beheld the whole commodiously. Perceiving that the troops would not attack them, except in words and menaces, they grew more violent, and furiously attempted to beat the doors in pieces with iron crows; placing ladders to the windows. In about a quarter of an hour, which gave time for the assembled magistrates to escape by a back door, they burst all open, and entered like a torrent with a universal shout of the spectators. From that moment, a shower of casements, sashes, shutters, chairs, tables, sofas, books, pictures, papers, etc. reigned incessantly from all the windows of the house, which is 70 or 80 feet long, and which was then succeeded by tiles, skirting-boards and every part of the building that force could detach. The troops, both foot and horse, were quiet spectators. . . . I remarked several common soldiers, with their white cockades among the plunderers, and instigating the mob even in sight of the officers of the detachment. There were amongst them people so decently dressed that I regarded them with no small surprise; they destroyed all the public archives; the streets for some way round strewed with papers. This has become a wanton mischief, for it will be the ruin of many families unconnected with the magistrates.

Arthur Young, op cit, pp 182–3

(d) A warning against disorder

Frenchmen, you destroy tyrants; your hate is frightening; it is shocking. . . . But you will be free! O my country, the rights of man will at last be respected among us! I know, O my fellow-

citizens, how deeply these turbulent scenes afflict your soul; like you, I am seized to the quick by such events; but think how ignominious it is to live and be a slave; think with what torments one
65 should punish crimes against humanity; think, finally, of what good, what satisfaction, what happiness awaits you, you and your children and your descendants, when august and blessed liberty will have set its temple among you! Yet do not forget that these proscriptions outrage humanity and make nature tremble.

Les Révolutions de Paris, No 2, 18–25 July 1789, Gilchrist and Murray, op cit, p 56

(e) The National Assembly's attitude

70 *10 August 1789* – The National Assembly, considering that the enemies of the nation, having lost hope of preventing by despotic violence the public regeneration and the establishment of liberty, appear to have conceived the criminal project of achieving the same purpose by the way of disorder and anarchy; that, among other
75 devices, they have, at the same time and almost in the same day, spread false alarms in the different provinces in the kingdom, and that in announcing incursions and plunderings which did not exist, have given way to excesses and crimes which threaten both property and persons, and which, menacing the universal order of society,
80 deserve the most severe punishment; that men have been audacious enough to issue false orders and even false edicts of the king, which have set one part of the nation against the other, at the very time when the National Assembly is putting forward decrees most favourably directed towards the interests of the people.

Procès-Verbal, No 46, J. M. Thompson (ed.), *French Revolution Documents* (1933), pp 55–6

Questions

a   What is there to indicate in extract *a* why the mobs destroyed the registers and archives of the castles and town halls as described in extracts *b* and *c*?

b   How did the Comte de Germiny deny that he had taken part in the eighteenth–century *réaction seigneuriale*?

c   For what different reasons did a revolutionary newspaper (extract *d*) and the National Assembly (extract *e*) condemn the popular violence?

★ d   To what extent did the French Revolution become a popular movement in the summer of 1789?

3   The Abolition of Feudal Rights

(a) The unforeseen future

Amid all the pleasures, we were drawing near to the month of August, laughing and dancing our way to the precipice. Thinking people were content to talk of abolishing all the abuses. France, they said, was about to be reborn. The word 'revolution' was never uttered. Had anyone dared to use it, he would have been thought mad. In the upper classes, this illusion of security misled the wise, who wanted to see an end to the abuses and to the waste of public money. This is why so many upright and honourable men, including the King himself who fully shared the illusion, hoped that they were about to enter a Golden Age. . . . People who frequented my aunt's company and my aunt herself were never at a loss for ideas for reforming abuses and for establishing a fairer distribution of taxes. People were particularly insistent on the need to base the new French Constitution on that of England, which very few people knew anything about.

Journal of Madame de la Tour du Pin, pp 78–9

(b) The night of 4 August (1)

I. The National Assembly destroys the feudal system entirely. It decrees that, in regard to rights and duties, both feudal and provincial, those relating to mortmain real or personal and to personal serfdom, and those which represent them, are abolished without indemnity; all the others are declared to be redeemable, and the price and method of redemption will be decided by the National Assembly. Those of the said rights, which are not suppressed by this decree, will continue nevertheless to be collected until there has been reimbursement.
III. The exclusive right of the chase and protected rabbit-warrens is abolished, and each landowner has the right to destroy and cause to be destroyed, solely on his own property, all sorts of game. . . .
IV. All seigneurial courts are suppressed without any indemnity; but nevertheless the officers of these courts will continue in their functions until the National Assembly has provided for the establishment of a new judicial system.
V. All forms of tithes and dues in place of them . . . are abolished, except for providing a means of defraying in another way, the expenses of divine worship, payment of priests, relief of the poor, repairing and rebuilding churches and presbyteries, and all the establishments, seminaries, schools, colleges, hospitals, monasteries and others, to which they are at present allocated. . . .
VII. Venality of judicial and municipal offices is suppressed forthwith. Justice will be administered freely. Nevertheless the officers administering these offices will continue to exercise their

functions and receive their emoluments until the Assembly has devised means to procure their reimbursement.

IX. Financial privileges, personal or real, in matters of taxation, are abolished forever. Payment will fall upon all citizens and all properties in the same manner and form. . . .

X. Since a national constitution and public liberty are more advantageous to the provinces than privileges which some enjoy, and which it is necessary to sacrifice for the close union of all parts of the empire, it is declared that all the special privileges of the provinces, principalities, lands, cantons, towns and villages, whether pecuniary or of any other sort, are abolished perpetually and remain included in the common rights of all Frenchmen.

XI. All citizens, without distinction of birth, may be admitted into all posts and dignities, whether ecclesiastical, civil or military, and no useful profession will carry loss of noble status.

Buchez and Roux, op cit, II, pp 259–62

(c) The night of 4 August (2)

Frenchmen are you not going to institute a fête in commemoration of that night when so many great things were done without the delays of scrutiny and as by inspiration? It is on that night, you must say, more than that of Holy Saturday, that we came forth from the wretched bondage of Egypt. That night put an end to the wild boars, rabbits and game devouring our crops. That night abolished the tithe and the fees of the clergy. . . . That night abolished taxes and exemptions. . . . That night has put down seigneurial justice and the free duchies, has abolished mortmain, corvée and crop-share rents, and effaced from the land of the Franks all traces of slavery. That night restored Frenchmen to the Rights of Man and declared all citizens equal, equally admissible to all offices, places and public employ; again, that night has snatched all civil offices, ecclesiastical and military, from wealth, birth and royalty, to give them to the nation as a whole on the basis of merit.

Discours de la Lanterne aux Parisiens, France, 1st Year of Liberty, pp 5–9, Gilchrist and Murray, op cit, pp 60–2

(d) The National Assembly denounced

Never mind, upon the views of the proposal for these articles which you are discussing to-day, the people of all the provinces regarded them as fully decreed; and they took every advantage which they alone can withdraw. They no longer pay taxes, they have armed themselves for smuggling; they have fixed the price of salt, and it is indeed happy that they have consented to pay a half of its former value; they have devastated the woods, countryside, estates, destroyed all the game and even ruined the crops at the very time when they have become most valuable to us. They refused to acknowledge rights whose abolition was still being discussed; they have ceased to fear the ministers of justice, whose abolition in the villages you have advised. They are acting, then, exactly as people who no longer fear the law, and it is the strongest who enjoy liberty, while your mission is to give it to the weak as well as to those who are powerful.

> *Le fouet national*, No I, 22 September 1789, p 3, Wickham Legg, *Select Documents*, I, pp 111–12

(e) A family ruined

The happenings of the night of 4th. August when, on the motion of the Vicomte de Noailles, feudal rights were abolished, should have convinced even the most incredulous that the National Assembly was unlikely to stop at this first measure of dispossession. The decree ruined my father-in-law, and our family fortunes never recovered from the effect of that night's session. . . . Since then we have been forced to continue a living, sometimes by the sale of the few possessions remaining to us, sometimes by taking salaried posts – though the salaries rarely covered the expense the posts involved. And so it is that, inch by inch, over a long period of years, we have gradually slid to the bottom of an abyss from which we shall not emerge in our generation.

> *Journal of Madame de la Tour du Pin*, p 93

Questions

a   To what extent did the peasant proprietors get what they wanted from the Revolution in 1789?

b   What is the meaning of the reference to 'Holy Saturday' and the 'wretched bondage of Egypt' in lines 59–60?

c   How were the nobility unexpectedly ruined on the night of 4 August?

d   'Four revolutions had already taken place in France by the end of August 1789' (Georges Lefebvre). Discuss this interpretation of the period from 1787 to 1789.

4   The October Days

(a) Fearful Paris

3 September 1789 – The National Assembly is in fear of Paris, and Paris is in fear of the forty or fifty thousand bandits who have installed themselves in Montmartre or the Palais Royal, and who have defied all attempts to bring them to order; now they continue to cause trouble. . . . The King will soon be unable to meet his commitments, and there is a threat of bankruptcy. The aristocracy is in despair, the clergy at the verge of frenzy, and the third estate is

completely dissatisfied. Only the ruling mob is content; They have
nothing to lose and only stand to gain. Nobody dares to give orders,
10 and nobody is willing to obey. This is France's present
freedom. . . . Many regiments mutinied, and some even threatened
their commanding officers with violence. . . . The Duke of Orleans
is strongly suspected of being the leader and instigator of the whole
business.

> Axel von Fersen, *Rescue the Queen, A Diary of the French
> Revolution 1789–93* (trans. Alfred Kurti, 1971), p 21

(b) Events at Versailles

15 *Versailles, 9 October 1789* – We have had dreadful doings. On the
6th., at night, a set of wretches forced themselves into the chateau,
screaming, '*La tête de la reine! à bas la reine! Louis ne sera plus roi – il nous
faut le Duc d'Orléans – il nous donnera du pain celui-là!*' Monsieur
Durepaire, one of the Gardes du Corps, defended the Queen's door
20 and was killed. Others took his place and were thrown down.
'*Sauvez la reine!*' was the cry of the Garde du Corps. Madame
Thibaud awoke the Queen, who threw a coverlid of the bed over her
and ran into the King's room, and, soon after she was gone, her door
was burst open. The King ran and fetched his son, and all together
25 they waited the event. They owed their rescue to M. de la Fayette
and the Gardes Françaises. He insisted upon the King taking up his
abode at Paris, without which he would not promise him safety. At
one, next day, therefore, they all went, partly escorted by the
poissardes [fishwomen] and their bullies. They were six hours going
30 from Versailles to Paris.

> Mrs Henry Swinburne to her husband, J. M. Thompson
> (ed), *English Witnesses of the French Revolution* (1938), pp 32–3

(c) The reception of the king (1)

The King, the Queen, the Daupin, etc., have arrived in the Capital at
seven o'clock in the evening. It is a happy day for the good Parisians
to possess at last their King. His presence will quickly change the face
of things; the poor will no longer die of hunger. But this good
35 fortune will soon vanish like a dream if we do not retain the presence
of the Royal Family among us until the constitution is completely
ready.

> *L'Ami du Peuple*, No XXVII, 6 October 1789, p 231,
> Wickham Legg, op cit, I, p 151

(d) The reception of the king (2)

The permanent residence of the King in Paris is a great event for all
the Citizens. It revives their confidence which had almost entirely
40 vanished; it restores the link between the Monarch and his Subjects.

It will recall a great number of fugitive families, who will gather the fruits of this new alliance. The humiliating barriers between the Throne and the Citizens will disappear; the ministerial despotism, which the royal absence seemed to encourage, will not be able to resist the vigilant eye of the Citizens who are always ready to reveal guilty conduct. May this happy day be the most brilliant epoch of our history, and show that the French people, so well-known for reverencing their Kings, have not degenerated, and even in the midst of revolutions preserve the same love and the same fidelity.

Le Fouet National, No IV, 13 October 1789, p 28, ibid, p 151

(e) The first emigrés (1)

My father-in-law's distaste for his Ministry [of War] increased daily. Nearly all the regiments of the army were in a state of revolt. Most of the officers, instead of opposing the efforts of the revolutionaries with a steady firmness, sent in their resignations and left France. To emigrate became a point of honour. Those who remained with their regiments or in their province received letters from émigré officers reproaching them for their cowardice and lack of loyalty to the royal family. Elderly gentlemen, who had returned to their manors, received through the post small parcels containing a white feather or an insulting caricature. It was an attempt to convince them that they had a duty to abandon their sovereign. They were promised the intervention of innumerable foreign armies.

Journal of Madame la Tour du Pin, p 125

(f) The first emigrés (2)

Everyone who was noble and loyal to his king felt that he was performing a duty. One could see old military men, peaceful people and heads of families, respond to this high-minded appeal and, without hesitation, leave the comforts of the foyer for the painful and adventurous life of a simple soldier. . . . It was very difficult to resist the pressure of public opinion. . . . One must leave or be dishonoured.

Alexandrine des Echerolles, *Une Femme Noble sous la Terreur* (1879), p 86 in Douglas Johnson (ed.), *French Society and the Revolution* (1976), p 136

Questions

a   Who were 'M. de la Fayette and the Gardes Françaises' (lines 25–6)?
b   Compare the different attitude towards the arrival of Louis XVI in Paris in extracts *c* and *d*.

   c   What difference did the flight of the émigrés make to the position of the monarchy in France?

★   *d*   What influence did the Duke of Orleans have upon the events of the Revolution?

V The Work of the Constituent Assembly October 1789– September 1791

Introduction

The Declaration of the Rights of Man was accepted by the Assembly on 26 August 1789 and proclaimed on 2 October. It laid down general principles typical of the eighteenth century, which were now to be those of the Revolution. Its denial of the system of privilege in the *ancien régime* was put into effect in local government and justice and the abolition of the nobility. Practically, finance presented the Assembly with a serious and immediate problem, which it met by issuing paper currency (assignats) and selling ecclesiastical property. The latter met with little opposition, but the subsequent Civil Constitution of the Clergy was accepted by only seven bishops and a third of the parochial clergy, and it was to prove the most divisive of all revolutionary legislation. The Voltairian members of the Assembly had not expected such opposition to the measure, but by the time the first revolutionary Constitution of 1791 was completed, counter-revolution had become a practical cause by having been given considerable popular support through the religious issue:

1 The debate among historians about the origins of the Declaration of Rights has been inconclusive. Thus, Alfred Cobban, *A History of Modern France* (1957), asserts that among the influences which produced it were 'not the little read and still less understood *Social Contract* of Rousseau,' but Norman Hampson, *Will and Circumstance: Montesquieu, Rousseau and the French Revolution* (1983), holds that it was 'faithful to what were believed to be Rousseau's ideas'. The extracts in this section provide some evidence relevant to the question.

2 The confiscation of ecclesiastical lands and the abolition of the nobility was a levelling measure in Church and State. By 1790 both bishops and noblemen had been deprived of their aristocratic status in the kingdom; but the ecclesiastical legislation received general support from the parish clergy. It had long been recognised that such reform was needed in the Church, which possessed nearly half the landed wealth of France; and while a bishop might have an annual income of 400,000 livres and an abbot 50,000 livres, a parish priest might get as little as 700 livres.

3 The Civil Constitution of the Clergy was regarded by its

promoters as a further measure of reform. It was imposed upon the Church, but the bishops would not have approved a measure which reduced both their privileges and the number of bishoprics. The opposition of most of them to it was swifter than that of the Pope, who was anxious about the future of the old papal territory of Avignon and delayed his decision for eight months.

4 By the time the Pope had issued a bull condemning the Constitution, the king had sanctioned it, and his remorse at having sinned in doing this was among the motives of his attempted flight from Paris. As shown by extracts in this section, this episode had serious consequences. Anti-monarchical feeling was strengthened in Paris, and the Austrian Emperor, believing that the royal family was threatened, issued the Declaration of Pilnitz, which, whatever its intentions, was provocative to France.

5 Most of the members of the Assembly wished to pass over quietly the king's action because they needed his participation in the new Constitution of 1791. His acceptance of it was secured, but its idea of a constitutional monarchy faced dislike from both royalists and republicans.

1   The Rights of Man

(a) The declaration of the Assembly, 2 October 1789

The National Assembly recognizes and declares in the presence and under the auspices of the Supreme Being, the following rights of man and the citizen:

1. Men are born free and remain free and equal in rights. Social distinctions can only be founded upon common usefulness.

2. The aim of every political association is the maintenance of the natural and inalienable rights of man. These rights are liberty, property, security and resistance to oppression.

3. The source of all sovereignty resides essentially in the nation. No group nor individual may exercise authority not derived expressly from it.

6. The law is the expression of the general will. All citizens have the right, personally or by their representatives, to agree in its establishment. It must be the same for all, whether it punishes or protects. All citizens, being equal in its eyes, are equally admissible to all dignities, offices and public employments, according to their ability and without any distinction than that of their virtues and talents.

16. Any society in which the guarantee of rights is not assured, nor the separation of powers determined, has not a constitution.

Faustin-Adolphe Hélie, *Les Constitutions de la France* (1880), pp 30–2

(b) Rousseau on the general will (1758)

The body politic is a moral being, possessed of a will, and this general will, which tends always to the preservation and welfare of the whole and of every part, and is the source of the laws, constitutes for all the members of the State, in their relations to one another and to it, the rule of what is just or unjust. . . . Every political society is composed of other smaller societies of various kinds, each of which has its interest and rules of conduct; but these societies, which everybody perceives, because they have an external or authorized form, are not the only ones that actually exist in the State; all individuals who are united by a common interest compose as many others, either temporary or permanent, whose interest is none the less real because it is less apparent. . . . The influence of all these tacit or formal associations causes by the influence of their will as many modifications of the public will. The will of these particular societies has always two relations; for the members of the association, it is a general will; for the great society, it is a particular will; and it is often right with regard to the first object and wrong to the second. The most general will is always the most just, and the voice of the people is, in fact, the voice of God.

> The Social Contract and Discourses by Jean-Jacques Rousseau (trans. G. D. H. Cole, Everyman Edition, 1938), pp. 253–4

(c) Montesquieu on the separation of powers (1748)

There are, in each State, three sorts of powers: the legislative power, the executive power of things which concern the rights of the people and the legislative power of that which concerns civil rights [the relations of the citizens with each other].

For the first, the prince or the magistrate makes temporary or permanent laws and amends or repeals those which are made. For the second, he makes peace or war, sends or receives ambassadors, establishes security and prevents invasions. For the third, he punishes crimes or judges different causes. . . . All will be lost if the same man or the same body of leaders, nobles or people exercise these three powers.

> Baron de Montesquieu, L'Esprit des Lois, Liv XI, Chap VI, Bayet and Albert, op cit, pp 34–5

(d) The American Declaration of Independence (1776)

We hold these truths to be self-evident, that all men are created equal, that they are endowed by their Creator with certain unalienable Rights; that among these are Life, Liberty and the pursuit of Happiness. That to secure these rights, Governments are instituted among Men, deriving their just powers from the consent of the governed. That whenever any Form of Government becomes

destructive of these ends, it is the Right of the People to alter or
abolish it, and to institute new Government, laying its foundations
on such principles and organizing its powers in such form, as to them
60 shall seem most likely to effect their Safety and Happiness.
G. M. Lamphere, *The United States Government* (1880), p 9

Questions

a Explain the reference to the Supreme Being in line 2.
b What aspects of the *ancien régime* were condemned in extract *a*?
c What did Rousseau, Montesquieu and the American Declaration
   of Independence contribute to the Declaration of Rights?
★ d Is it true that in the history of ideas the Declaration of Rights
      belongs to the past rather than to the future?

2 The Clergy and the Nobility

(a) The confiscation of the Church lands, 2 November 1789

I. The National Assembly declares that all ecclesiastical property is
at the disposition of the nation for the purpose of providing, in a
suitable manner, for the conduct of worship, the maintenance of the
clergy and the relief of the poor under the supervision and following
5 instructions from the Provinces.
   II. That in the arrangements made for the maintenance of the
ministers of religion, each shall be assured of an endowment for his
cure of not less than 1200 livres a year, not including his lodging and
accompanying garden.
Procès-Verbal, No CXIV, 2 November 1789, p 4

(b) The abolition of the nobility, 20 July 1790

10 I. The National Assembly decrees that the hereditary nobility is
abolished forever; in consequence the titles of *prince, duc, comte,
marquis, vicomte, baron, chevalier, messire, écuyer, noble* and all other
similar titles shall not be assumed or given to anyone.
   II. Any French citizen may only use the true name of his family;
15 he may no longer wear livery or cause it to be worn nor have a coat of
arms; incense will be burned in church only to honour the Deity and
not offered to anyone whoever he may be.
   III. The titles of *monseigneur* and *messeigneurs* will not be given to
any group or individual, as well as the titles of *excellence, altesse,*
20 *eminence* or *grandeur.* . . .
Archives parlementaires, XVI, p 378

(c) The confiscation justified

Every body politic in a nation cannot exist on its own. It cannot possess, as a legal owner, a large amount of independent wealth, without becoming a sucker which, in living upon the sap, wastes away and weakens the tree which gave it birth; this truth is simple, natural and obvious, the clergy have nothing to oppose to it which could destroy or diminish it in the eyes of those who think.

> *Chronique de Paris*, No LXX, 1 November 1789, p 280, col 1

(d) The virtues of the nobility and clergy

Country folk, see what a future has been left to you. These nobles, in whose homes you used to shelter from the season's inclemency, you pursued from refuge to refuge; will you dare to ask them for bread, when you have not left them asylum? Those pastors, who lived with you, and through whom you lived, are now on wages; and one day perhaps, deprived even of this income, they will not have, like you, the spade and plough to fall back upon. Yet we now hear you slandering them; for you are daily being taught to become more unjust. They will have been deprived of the means of helping you, yet you will accuse them of being indifferent to your sufferings, when they are beggars like you. Your injustice will be the most severe of their punishments; and the most sacred, the most noble of callings will become the saddest and most wretched of these estates.

> Pierre-Barnabé Durosoi, *La Gazette de Paris*, 30 March 1790,
> Gilchrist and Murray, op cit, p 89

(e) A threat to the monarchy

Almost all the great men, the most virtuous men who have lived among all peoples, have unanimously recognized as a constitutional principle that it is not possible to have a Monarchy without a Nobility; since the hereditary Nobility has been *abolished forever* by the decree passed in this session, one must draw from it the consequences of the principle established by all writers, legislators, philosophers and moralists revered in all nations.

Louis XIV, in the days of his glory, said: *there are no more Pyrenees*; Voltaire, ready to go down into his tomb said: *there is no more Versailles*; from Saturday evening, Louis XVI can say: *no more Monarchy*.

> *Chronique de Paris*, No LXXII, 23 June 1790, p 1, col 1

Questions

a   What is there to suggest in extract *a* that the Assembly did not wish to alienate the parochial clergy?

b   What differing view of the place of the clergy in the French nation is taken in extracts *c* and *d*?

c   Why should it be thought that the abolition of the nobility meant the abolition of the monarchy?

d 'If this uniform surface is favourable to liberty, it also facilitates the exercise of power' (Mirabeau). Discuss this comment upon the laws confiscating Church property and abolishing the nobility.

3 The Reorganisation of the Church

(a) *The Civil Constitution of the Clergy, 12 July 1790*

FIRST SECTION – CONCERNING ECCLESIASTICAL
OFFICES

I. Each department shall form a single diocese, and each diocese shall have the same area and the same boundaries as the department.

5   IV. It is forbidden to every church or parish in France and to all French citizens to recognize in any matter and under any pretext whatsoever the authority of an ordinary or metropolitan bishop whose see may be established under the domination of a foreign power, nor that of his delegates, residing in France or elsewhere: all

10 this to be without prejudice to the unity of the faith and the unity which will be maintained with the visible Head of the universal church.

SECOND SECTION – NOMINATION TO
ECCLESIASTICAL BENEFICES

15   IV. Upon the first intimation that the procurator-general-syndic of the department receives of the vacancy of an episcopal see, by death, translation or other cause, he shall give notice to the procurator-syndics of the districts to summon the electors who will have taken part in the most recent nomination of the departmental

20 officials to choose a new bishop.

XIX. The new bishop shall not address himself to the Pope to obtain any confirmation of his election; but he shall write to him as the visible head of the universal church to witness to the unity of the faith and the communion which he should maintain with him.

25   XXI. Before the ceremony of his consecration begins, the elected bishop shall swear, in the presence of the municipal officers, the people and the clergy, a solemn oath to attend with care to the people of the diocese entrusted to him, to be faithful to the nation, the law and the King and to maintain with all his power the constitution

30 decreed by the National Assembly and accepted by the King.

XXVI. The body of electors empowered to nominate to parishes shall always be formed from those who nominate the district officials. . . .

XXVIII. The elected and instituted parish priests shall take the

35 same oath as the bishops in their church on a Sunday, before the parish mass, in the presence of the municipal officers of the place, the people and the clergy; until then they shall not be able to undertake any parochial function.

    J. M. Roberts, *French Revolution Documents*, pp 225–30

70   THE FRENCH REVOLUTION

(b) The oath required at confirmation in Vienne diocese

In order not to separate myself from the faith of my fathers, but to live in their religion until death, I will remain inviolably attached and submit to Our Holy Father the Pope, Vicar of Jesus Christ, successor of Saint Peter, and consequently the head of this holy religion, to Mgr. d'Aviau, Archbishop of Vienne and his rightful successors; I will not recognize any priest who does not hold from them his position and his powers; this is why I will continue to ignore in religious matters all those who, by their oath to the Civil Constitution of the Clergy, their refusal to retract in the meanwhile, their temerity in performing their functions despite the Pope's injunction, have removed themselves from communion with him; never will I go to their mass; never will receive from them the sacrament; never, in a word, will I communicate with them in spiritual matters.

> A. Latreille, *L'Eglise Catholique et la Révolution française* (2 vols, 1946–50), I, p 217

(c) Liberty and true religion

What then is a priest? He is a citizen who, feeling himself endowed with gentleness and humility, consecrates himself in a special fashion to the cult of those virtues that tend towards the good of society. . . . Under the old régime and in times when we lacked energy, a good priest would ease our chains and give us hope that sooner or later God, who had called us all to liberty, would give us the opportunity and provide us with the means for breaking our chains. In this way Moses and Aaron were truly citizen-priests, since they restored the courage of their downtrodden countrymen, since they led them to a holy insurrection and finally to cast off the yoke of the Egyptian aristocracy. . . .

My friends, my brothers! Three more months, and the country will be saved. Have patience; take courage; the beginnings of liberty are not at all easy; put on a good face; let harmony reign in our midst. Let us remain united, and we shall stay free. Do not let the refusal of a few bishops and several priests [to take the oath] alarm you; that is their affair. God is on our side, for liberty is his beloved daughter. Liberty is the handmaid of religion. God repulses the incense of slaves. Servitude gives rise only to superstition. Let us then remain free to please God and to make ourselves respected among men.

> *Les Révolutions de Paris*, No 79, 8–15 January 1791, pp 16–17, Gilchrist and Murray, op cit, p 91

(d) The Pope's exhortation to the faithful

Finally we entreat you in the Lord, beloved Catholic children, all who are in the kingdom of France, we urge you from the depth of

75 our heart to remember the religion and faith of your fathers, do not
forsake this one and true religion, which bestows the gift of eternal
life, which preserves and prospers civil societies. Take diligent care
not to listen to the insidious voices of the philsophers of this age,
which bring death; and shun all usurpers, whether they are called
80 archbishops, bishops or parochial clergy, that you have nothing in
common with them, especially in divine matters; listen carefully to
the voices of your rightful pastors, who live as those lawfully set
over you for the future; adhere to Our word alone: for no one can
remain within the Church of Christ, unless he unites himself with its
85 visible head and stands before the throne of Peter. Above all, that
everyone may be inspired fervently to fulfil their duty, We ask our
heavenly Father to grant you the spirit of counsel, truth and
constancy, as a pledge of his eternal care for you, Our beloved
children; and honoured brethren and beloved children, may the
90 apostolic blessing remain with you always.

> *Bull of Pius VI Condemning the Oath of the Civil Constitution of
> the Clergy*, 13 April 1791, Wickham Legg, *Select Documents*,
> II, pp 209–10

Questions

a Explain the phrase 'under the domination of a foreign power'
(lines 8–9).

b Why were faithful members of the Church expected not to
recognise the constituent clergy?

c How did revolutionary opinion think a 'citizen-priest' should
serve the people?

★ d Why did the Civil Constitution of the Clergy arouse more
hostility in France than the confiscation of the Church lands?

4 The Flight to Varennes, 21 June 1791

(a) A royal escape?

8 March 1791 – the King's party consists of utterly incompetent
people, or of those whose attitude is so exaggerated and outraged
that they can neither be swayed nor trusted, which means that
matters proceed slowly and with the utmost precautions. The same
5 applies to finding somewhere to which the King could escape. One
would really have to be certain of it, and to have found a devoted and
competent man who knows the troops and could influence them.
But all this would be inadequate without the support of France's
neighbours, Spain and Switzerland, and of the Emperor; the Nordic
10 states must keep Britain, Prussia and Holland in check to make sure
that they do not obstruct the good intentions of the other powers and

prevent any efforts to help the King of France. Without such joint efforts, the King of France, I am afraid, will never regain his authority.

Axel von Fersen, *Rescue the Queen*, pp 23–4

(b) The king's intentions

The King, who had read a lot of history and during the Revolution preferred to read that of England, had remarked that James II had lost the throne because he left his kingdom and that Charles I's death-sentence had been grounded on the fact that he had levied war on his subjects. These reflections, which he often communicated to me, instilled in him an extreme repugnance to leaving France to put himself at the head of his troops or to cause them to move against his revolted peoples.

I never knew what course the King would have adopted at Montmédy and what would have been his conduct in relation to the Assembly in such difficult circumstances. Anyone who knew the King's religious character could not doubt that in taking his oath [to uphold the Constitution], his intention was to observe [the Constitution] scrupulously and execute the laws which it contained. . . . But this Constitution was then so imperfect; it was not finished; every day it became more vicious and impossible to uphold and implement. . . . I had, therefore, to suppose that once the King had recovered his liberty, he would have based his conduct on the dispositions of the people and of the army and that he would only have employed force in the eventuality of his not having been able to come to a suitable arrangement with the Assembly, which several leading members of the Assembly – including Mirabeau, Duport and even the Lameths – desired, realizing all the vices of their constitution, which tended towards a republic they did not want and anarchy which they dreaded.

Memoires du Marquis de Bouillé (ed. M. F. Barrière, 1859), pp 223–4, John Hardman, *The French Revolution*, p 123

(c) The royal return, 25 June 1791

We will content ourselves with saying, up to to-day, that surrounded by a barrier formed of five hundred thousand citizens, of whom a large number were armed, Louis XVI, his wife and his sister arrived at the Tuileries between seven and half-past. No sign of disapproval, no apparent sign of contempt escaped from the numerous gathering. It was confined to denying any military honours to these fugitives. They were received with grounded arms. All the citizens kept their hats on their heads as if in common agreement.

Courrier des LXXXIII Départements, vol XXV, no XXVI, p 396

(d) The Declaration of Pilnitz, 27 August 1791

His Majesty the Emperor and His Majesty the King of Prussia,
50 having heard the wishes and representations of Monsieur and of the
Comte d'Artois, jointly declare that they regard the present situation
of the King of France as an object of interest to all the sovereigns of
Europe. They hope that this interest will not fail to be recognized by
the powers whose help is entreated, and that consequently they will
55 not refuse to employ, jointly with their above-mentioned Majesties,
the most effective means, relative to their forces, to place the King of
France in a position to establish, with perfect freedom, the basis of a
monarchical government equally agreeable to the rights of
sovereigns and the well-being of the French nation. If this is so,
60 Their Majesties the Emperor and the King of Prussia are resolved to
act promptly, in common accord, with the forces necessary to
achieve their proposed, mutual purpose. Meanwhile, they will give
to their troops such orders as are necessary to enable them to put this
into effect.

Wickham Legg, *Select Documents*, II, p 127

Questions

a   Who were 'Monsieur' and 'the Comte d'Artois' (lines 50–1)?

b   Were Count von Fersen and Louis XVI in agreement about the
purpose of the royal flight from Paris?

c   Why should the contents of the Declaration of Pilnitz have caused
Marie Antoinette to say, 'The Emperor has betrayed us'?

★ d   In what way was the flight to Varennes a turning-point in the
history of the Revolution?

5   The Constitution of 14 September 1791

(a) Constitutional articles

1. All the powers [executive, legislative and judicial] emanate
entirely and can only emanate from the nation.

2. The government of France is monarchical; no authority in
France is above the law by which alone the King reigns, and it is only
5   in the name of the law that he can require obedience.

3. The National Assembly has declared and recognized as
fundamental elements in the French monarchy that the King's
person is inviolable and sacred; that the throne is indivisible and that
the crown is hereditary in the ruling dynasty from male to male in
10   order of primogeniture to the perpetual and absolute exclusion of
females and their descendants. . . .

4. The National Assembly will be a permanent institution.

5. The National Assembly will be composed of only one
chamber.

6. Each parliament will last for two years.

7. At the end of each parliament, elections will be held for every seat.

8. The legislative power resides in the National Assembly which shall exercise it as follows:

9. No act of the legislative body may be considered a law unless it has been passed by the freely and legally elected representatives of the nation and received the royal assent.

10. The King may refuse his assent to acts of the legislative body.

11. If the King refuses his assent, this veto will be only suspensive.

12. The King's suspensive veto will end with the second parliament following that proposing the law.

13. The King may invite the National Assembly to take a matter into consideration, but the initiation of legislation appertains exclusively to the representatives of the nation.

14. The creation and abolition of offices can operate only in virtue of an act of the legislative body sanctioned by the King.

15. No tax or levy, whether in kind or money, nor any loan, direct or indirect, may be raised except by an implicit decree of the assembly of the representatives of the nation.

16. The executive power resides exclusively in the King's hands.

17. The executive power may not issue any laws, even provisional ones, but merely proclamations conformable with the laws to order or bring their observance.

18. The ministers and other agents of the executive are responsible for their use of the funds of the department and likewise for such infringements of the law as they may commit, whatever orders they may have received. But no order of the King's may be executed without its having been signed by His Majesty and countersigned by a Secretary of State.

19. The judicial power may in no case be exercised by the King or by the legislative body, but justice shall be exercised, in the name of the King, exclusively by the tribunals established by law in conformity with the principles of the Constitution and the forms prescribed by law.

Archives parlementaires, IX, pp 236–7, John Hardman, op cit, pp 116–17

(b) The king's acceptance of the Constitution

An usher announced the King. The Assembly rose, most of the right having departed. His Majesty entered, was placed on the President's left and said:

'Gentlemen, I come to consecrate solemnly here the acceptance which I have given to the constitutional act. Consequently I swear to be faithful to the nation and the law; to use all the power bestowed

upon me to maintain the constitution decreed by the National
Constituent Assembly and to execute the laws. May this great and
memorable occasion re-establish peace and unity and become the
60 pledge of the happiness of the people and the prosperity of the
empire.'
    At the moment that the King spoke the words: 'I swear to be
faithful to the nation,' the Assembly sat, and for the first time in the
life of Louis XVI, for the first time since the foundation of the
65 monarchy, the King of France stood to swear fidelity to his seated
subjects; but they, having become sovereign, saw the King as no
more than their chief salaried official, legally liable to dethronement.
After the words: 'National Constituent Assembly,' the King, seeing
that he alone was standing, looked round the chamber with a gaze in
70 which graciousness was tempered by surprise, and His Majesty sat
and continued his speech.
        Mercure de France, 14 September 1791, p 296

(c) The king's reason for acceptance

I have carefully weighed the matter and concluded that war presents
no other advantages but horrors and a continuance of discord. I have
therefore thought that this idea should be set aside and that I should
75 try once more the sole means remaining to me, namely the junction
of my will to the principles of the Constitution. I realize all the
difficulties of governing a large nation in this way – indeed I will say
that I realize it is impossible. But the obstacles that I would have put
in the way [by refusing to accept the Constitution] would have
80 brought about the war I sought to avoid and would have prevented
the people from properly assessing the Constitution because it
would only have seen my constant opposition. By my adopting its
principles executing them in good faith, they will come to know the
cause of their misfortunes; public opinion will change; and since,
85 without this change, I could only expect new convulsions, I . . .
[considered] that I would be proceeding towards a better order by
my acceptance than by my refusal.
        Feuillet de Conches, *Louis XVI*, II, p 375, John Hardman, op
        cit, p 138

Questions

a   What can be learnt from extracts *a* and *b* about the intended role
    of the king in the Constitution?
b   Why were 'most of the right' (line 51) absent from the
    Constituent Assembly when the king accepted the Constitution?
c   Was Louis XVI's reason for accepting the Constitution
    consistent with his intentions when fleeing from Paris earlier in
    the year (pp 73 and 76)?

d 'The Constitution was a veritable monster: there was too much republic for a monarchy and too much monarchy for a republic' (Etienne Dumont). Discuss this judgement.

VI The Legislative Assembly and the Fall of the Monarchy October 1791–September 1792

Introduction

Under the Constitution, the Constituent Assembly was replaced by the Legislative Assembly in which the lead among the republicans was taken by a group known as the Brissotins (after their leader, Jacques Pierre Brissotin), but later as the Girondins. They brought about a declaration of war against Austria in April 1792. The opening disasters suffered by France and the threatening manifesto issued by the Prussian commander, the Duke of Brunswick, set off disturbances in Paris. On 10 August the royal palace of the Tuileries was attacked, and three days later the royal family was imprisoned in the Temple. The invading enemy forces gained further victories on French territory, and the September Massacres in the Paris prisons followed. The Assembly had clearly lost control of events, and the short-lived Constitution had failed. The Girondins perpetuated their hold on power by summoning a National Convention, to be elected by universal suffrage, for the purpose of drawing up a new constitution. This met on 20 September; it abolished the monarchy and henceforward dated its decrees from the first year of the Republic:

1 Whatever might be the actual situation, popular opinion regarded the émigrés as presenting France with a dangerous threat of foreign invasion and aristocratic rebellion. The Girondins were ready to gain a reputation for patriotism by supporting the cry for war. P-V. Vergniaud, one of the greatest of the Girondin orators in the Assembly, urged a preventive war against the émigrés; but Maximilien Robespierre was among the few who opposed this because it might play into the hands of the king. When war was declared on Austria, it was chiefly because the emperor was alleged to have refused to disperse the concentrations of armed émigrés within the Empire, but it was also represented as a new kind of war, undertaken not only to protect France's newly-gained liberties, but in addition as a military crusade to promote the cause of revolution abroad among peoples who had not yet overthrown their despotic rulers and gained their freedom.

2 As the war opened badly for France, the Girondins found themselves threatened by what they had done. They sought to

distract popular condemnation of their failure by encouraging hostility against the monarchy. Jean-Marie Roland, the incompetent Minister of the Interior, wrote a letter, actually composed by Madame Roland, indicting the king for his alleged failure to observe the Constitution and suggesting the possibility of revolutionary violence. Louis dismissed Roland and his two chief supporters in the ministry. The action of the Girondins merely increased popular unrest. In June a crowd penetrated the Tuileries, and Louis probably owed his life to his composure during the episode. The situation was worsened by the issue of the Brunswick Manifesto, and a revolt was clearly imminent in Paris.

3 The Girondins, who had been exploiting the situation in their own interests, now found that they were in danger of being overwhelmed by it. Vergniaud and other leaders attempted to save the monarchical constitution; but the Mauconseil Section of Paris called for the deposition of the king. The rising of 10 August was of great significance. It was no less than a second revolution, which, in effect, inaugurated the Republic. The Girondins were helpless spectators during the subsequent September Massacres, but the extracts in this section show with what rapidity they acted in the Convention to bring about the constitutional change in France.

1 The Coming of War

(a) The émigrés and France

There is much talk of the two letters to the King published under the name of the French princes who are in Germany. One, it is said, was written by the King's two brothers, the other by the three princes of the house of Condé. The declaration of the sovereigns assembled at Pilnitz is linked with these documents, which have no other claim to authenticity. However that may be, rumours of war grow less each day. It is generally believed that a league of all the rulers of Europe against French freedom is morally impossible. . . . It is also said that war, if it takes place, will not break out before next spring, and that then the last Frenchman will die rather than be subjected to the laws of foreign powers. The confidence that the King displays towards the people, since his acceptance of the Constitution revives their hopes and doubles their courage.

>   *Babillard*, no. CI, 22 September 1791, p 506

(b) The émigrés and the emperor

Joseph-François de Rigaud, Comte de Vaudreuil to Charles Philippe de Bourbon, Comte d'Artois, from Vienna, 28 October 1791 – My conversation with the Emperor was not lengthy; but I had time to tell him that ten thousand exiled gentlemen, lacking help, would be

forced by necessity to support themselves by the sword, and that it
would be impossible to condemn as foolish those driven to this
20   despair and absolute necessity; that the Princes undoubtedly share
the lot and the perils of all these faithful nobility; that they have
nevertheless demonstrated to everyone their patience and prudence,
and that an opportunity would soon come for them to display their
courage; and that any mishaps which might result from this situation
25   must not be attributed to them. I then spoke of the trouble which
would result from such an immediate occurrence.

The Emperor spoke to me of the prodigious emigration since the
King's acceptance of the Constitution and asked me if it were true
that many bourgeois wished also to emigrate.
30   I replied that nothing was more true and that the Princes lack both
territory and money to maintain them as well as several faithful
regiments.

He made no reply to this.

I said that the response of the Princes to all those who wished to
35   emigrate was that, if they were safe at home and could be useful
there, they should stay there; but if they were in danger and without
means of serving the King at home, they must leave and join the
Princes.

The Emperor agree that this response is just and wise.

Correspondance intime du Comte de Vaudreuil et du Comte d'Artois
(ed. L. Pingaud, 2 vols, 1962), II, pp 38–9

(c) The call for war

40   *Pierre-Victurien Vergniaud to the Diplomatic Committe, 18 January 1792*
– I wish to speak to you concerning the émigrés. Have you heard it
said that they are at Coblenz? Citizens without number must hasten
to fight them. Are they gathered on the banks of the Rhine? You
must garrison your frontiers with two army corps. Do
45   neighbouring powers afford them refuge? You must resolve to make
an attack on them. Have you heard, on the contrary, that they are in
the depths of Germany? You can lay down arms. Are they preparing
a new offensive against you? Your anger returns. Are they
distracting you with fine promises? You can disarm again. So, it is
50   the émigrés and their advisers by their attitude towards you who are
your leaders, disposing of your armies and resources; they are the
arbiters of your peace and your destiny. It is for you to decide
whether this humiliating role is worthy of a great people.

H. Morse Stephens (ed.), *The Principal Speeches of the
Statesmen and Orators of the French Revolution* (2 vols, 1892), I,
p 284

(d) Opposition to war

Maximilien Robespierre to the Jacobin Club, 2 January 1792 – Of the two opinions which are balanced in this assembly, one claims all the ideas which stimulate the imagination, all the shining hopes which arouse enthusiasm, and even a generous sentiment upheld by all the most active and powerful means that the government can employ to influence opinion; the other rests solely upon cold reason and sad truth. To be popular, one must defend the first; to be realistic, one must uphold the second with the certainty of displeasing all those who have the power to do harm – I declare myself for that. . . .

The court and the factions have no doubt reasons for adopting their plan for war; what should be ours? 'The honour of the French name,' you say. Good heavens, the French nation dishonoured by this mob of fugitives, as ridiculous as powerless, that it can despoil of its possessions and mark, in the eyes of the world, with the brand of crime and treason! Ah! the shame consists in being deceived by the unscrupulous artifices of the enemies of our liberty. Magnanimity, wisdom, liberty, fortune, virtue, there is our honour. What you wish to revive is the soul, the support of despotism; it is the honour of aristocracy's heroes, of all tyrants; it is the honour of crime, it is a strange being which I believe is born by I know not what monstrous union of vice and virtue, but is allied with the first to destroy its mother; it is prescribed in the land of liberty: leave this honour alone or send it beyond the Rhine, where it may seek a refuge in the heart or head of the princes and gentlemen of Coblenz.

Ibid, II, pp 306–16

(e) The declaration of war on Austria, 29 April 1792

The National Assembly, deliberating on the formal proposal of the King, considering that the court of Vienna, in contempt of treaties, has not ceased to offer open protection to French rebels, that it has initiated and formed a concert with several European powers against the independence and security of the French nation. . . .

That despite the proposal made to him [the Emperor] in the note of 11 March 1792 that both nations should reduce the troops on their frontiers to their peace-time effectives, he has continued and increased his warlike preparations.

That he has formally infringed the sovereignty of the French nation in declaring his wish to uphold the claims of the German princes with possessions in France to whom the French nation has continually offered compensation.

That he has sought to divide French citizens and arm them against each other by offering the malcontents a place in the concert of powers. . . .

The National Assembly declares that the French nation, faithful to the principles enshrined in the Constitution 'not to undertake any war with the aim of making conquests and never to employ its forces against the liberty of any people,' only takes up arms to maintain its liberty and independence; that the war it is obliged to conduct is not a war of nation against nation, but the just defence of a free people against the unjust aggression of a king.

100

That the French will never confuse their brothers with their real enemies; that they will neglect nothing to alleviate the scourge of war, to spare and preserve property, and to visit all the misfortune inseparable from war on those alone who conspire against her liberty.

105

That the French nation adopts in advance all foreigners who, renouncing the cause of her enemies, come to range themselves under her banners and devote their efforts to the defence of her liberty; that it will even assist, by all means in its power, their establishment in France.

110

Archives parlementaires, XLII, pp 217–18

Questions

a Does the newspaper account in extract *a* correctly forecast why French opinion was to be swayed in favour of war?

b Do you consider, from extracts *b*, *c* and *d*, that the émigrés were or were not a real danger to France?

c What is the meaning of the reference to 'the court and the factions' (line 63)?

★ d 'No one loves armed missionaries' (Robespierre). Account for the failure of the French to wage 'a war of peoples against kings'.

2   The Summer of 1792

(a) Jean-Marie Roland to the king, 10 June 1792

Sire: the present condition of France cannot last long; it is a state of crisis, the violence of which is reaching its height; it must be ended by a measure which should interest your Majesty as much as it concerns the whole realm. . . .

5

The French people have given themselves a Constitution; it has produced malcontents and rebels; the majority of the nation wishes to maintain it; it has sworn to defend it at the price of its blood, and it has greeted with joy the war which offered a great opportunity to guarantee it. The minority, however, sustained by hope, has united all its efforts to gain an advantage. Hence this internal struggle against the laws, this anarchy which good citizens lament, and of which malevolent persons are careful to avail themselves in order to calumniate the new regime. . . .

10

Devotion to the Constitution has increased; not only did the people owe it obvious benefits, but they thought it would bring them greater ones. . . . The Declaration of Rights has become a political gospel, and the French constitution a religion, for which the people are ready to perish. . . .

15

Two important decrees have been passed; both intimately concern public tranquillity and the safety of the State. The vetoing of their enactment arouses mistrust; if it is continued, it will cause discontent; and I dare say that, in the general stirring of passions, the malcontents will be able to carry all with them. . . .

I know that the austere language of truth is rarely welcomed at the throne; I know also that it is because it almost never makes itself heard there that revolutions become necessary; I know above all that I must speak to your Majesty, not only as a citizen subject to the law, but as a minister honoured with his confidence or invested with duties which imply it; and I know nothing that can hinder me from fulfilling a duty of which I am aware.

Ibid, XLV, pp 163–4

(b) The attack on the Tuileries, 20 June 1792

22 June 1792 – The late attempt of the Jacobins to intimidate His Most Christian Majesty has failed entirely and has served only to impress more strongly on the minds of those who wish for order and good government an abhorrence of their principles and practices. The majesty of the throne was sullied, but it gave the King a happy opportunity of displaying an extraordinary degree of calmness and courage, which may be of infinite service. The circumstances of his having applied the hand of a grenadier to his heart, saying, 'feel here if there are any signs of fear,' is perfectly true. . . .

The King, finding the mob determined to force the door of the antechamber of his apartment, ordered his attendants to withdraw and placed himself in the recess of one of the windows, where, attended by a few grenadiers, he suffered the mob to approach him, accepted from them a red cap with tricolor ribands which he wore during the whole time that they remained in the palace, and, upon their expressing a wish that he should drink to the health of the nation, His Majesty condescended to comply with their request and drunk the remains of some wine in a cup, out of which a grenadier had previously drunk.

The Despatches of Earl Gower, British Ambassador at Paris (ed. Oscar Browning, 1885), pp 193–4

(c) The king disparaged

Pierre-Victurien Vergniaud to the National Assembly, 3 July 1792 – It is *in the name of the King* that the French princes have tried to rouse all the courts of Europe against the nation; it is *to uphold the dignity of the King* that the Declaration of Pilnitz was made and the monstrous alliance between the courts of Vienna and Berlin formed; it is *to defend the King* that the former companies of the royal guard are to be seen formed in Germany under the flag of rebellion; it is *to come to the help of the King* that the émigrés seek and obtain employment in the

Austrian armies and make ready to tear out the heart of their native country; it is to join these valiant knights of the *royal prerogative* that other most honourable and fine gentlemen abandon their post in the presence of the enemy, break their oaths, steal the funds, labour to corrupt their soldiers and so glorying in cowardice, perjury, bribery, theft and murder; it is against the nation or the National Assembly alone and *to maintain the splendour of the throne* that the King of Bohemia and Hungary [the Emperor] makes war on us, and the King of Prussia marches towards our frontiers; it is *in the name of the King* that liberty is attacked and that, if they are not driven back, they will soon dismember the state to reward with its wealth the allied powers; for we understand the generosity of kings, we know with what disinterestedness they send their armies to lay waste a foreign country, and at what point we can believe that they will exhaust their treasure to sustain a war that cannot be profitable for them. And finally, it is *the name of the King* which is the pretext or cause of all the evils which seek to pile up on our heads, and which we have to dread.

Morse Stephens, op cit, I, pp 306–7

(d) The Brunswick Manifesto, 25 July 1792

Convinced that the sober part of the [French] nation detest the excesses of a faction which has enslaved them, and that the majority of the inhabitants wait with impatience the moment when succours shall arrive, to declare themselves openly against the odious enterprises of their oppressors – his Majesty the Emperor and his Majesty the King of Prussia earnestly invite them to return without delay into the paths of reason and justice, of order and peace.

It is with this view that I, the under-signed, General Commandant in Chief of the two armies, do declare –

1. That, drawn into the present war by irresistible circumstances, the two allied courts have no other object in view than the welfare of France, without any pretence to enrich themselves by making conquests.

2. That they do not mean to meddle with the internal government of France, but that they firmly intend to deliver the King, the Queen, and the royal family, from their captivity, and to ensure to his Most Christian Majesty that safety which is necessary for his making, without danger and without obstacles, such convocations as he shall judge proper, and for endeavouring to ensure the welfare of his subjects, according to his promises, and to the utmost of his power.

8. The city of Paris and all its inhabitants without distinction, shall be called upon to submit instantly and without delay to the King, to set that prince at full liberty, and to ensure to his, and to all the royal persons, that inviolability and respect which are due by the laws of nature and of nations to sovereigns; their Imperial and Royal Majesties making personally responsible for all events, on pain of

losing their heads, pursuant to military trials, without hopes of pardon, all the members of the National Assembly, of the department of the district, of the municipality, and of the national guards of Paris, justices of peace, and others whom it may concern; and their Imperial and Royal Majesties further declare, on their faith and word of Emperor and King, that if the palace of Tuileries be forced or insulted; if the least violence be offered, the least outrage done to their Majesties the King, the Queen, and the Royal family; if they be not immediately placed in safety and set at liberty, they will inflict on those who shall deserve it, the most exemplary and every memorable avenging punishments, by giving up the city of Paris to military execution, and exposing it to total destruction; and the rebels who shall be guilty of illegal resistance shall suffer the punishments which they shall have deserved.

Translation in *Annual Register*, London 1792, pp 229–31

Questions

a   What were the two decrees, mentioned in line 19, which were vetoed by the king?
b   What is there in extract *b* to suggest the reason for Vergniaud's wish to discredit the king in extract *c*?
c   Why did the demonstration of 20 June take place?
d   Was the Brunswick Manifesto the final incident which precipitated the downfall of the king?

3   The Dethronement of Louis XVI

(a) A memorandum by Vergniaud

The King has been cruelly deceived if he has been led to believe that not to deviate from the line of constitutional rectitude is to do all that he should. Merely not to infringe the Constitution is nothing. His oaths also impose on him the duty to defend it: he would be betraying it no less by a policy of inactivity than by explicit collusion with the coalition powers. These two crimes would be equal in the eyes of the nation; it would judge them with the same severity.

John Hardman, op cit, p 144

(b) The address of the Section Mauconseil to Parisians

31 July 1792 – The citizens of the Section Mauconseil have undertaken the noble design of regaining their rights and securing the triumph of liberty or burying themselves in its ruins; and doubtless this inspiring example will be imitated by all the sections of the State that Paris may still amaze the universe and dismay despotism.

For too long a wretched tyrant has played with our destiny; let us

15 not delay to punish him lest he gains his triumph; citizens, arise and
    ensure that a tyrant is never pardoned. Without any longer diverting
    ourselves by considering his errors, crimes and falsehoods, let us
    strike the fearful colossus of despotism, so that he falls and is broken
    in pieces and that the sound of his fall alarms tyrants throughout the
20 world.
        Let us all unite to pronounce the deposition of this cruel king. Let
    us say with one accord: *Louis XVI is no longer King of the French.*
    Public opinion alone gives kings their power. Very well! Citizens,
    employ opinion to depose him, for public opinion makes and
25 unmakes kings. Louis XVI has earned the most disgraceful
    condemnation. All parties in the State vehemently disavow him; but
    none of them has openly expressed his attitude.
        The Section Mauconseil declares therefore to all the parties that, in
    considering vows in general, *it no longer recognizes Louis XVI as King*
30 *of the French*, and it abjures the vow that it took to be faithful to him,
    since it was mistaken in its faith. Perjury is a virtue when a crime is
    threatened.
        Citizens, follow our example. Tyranny falls, and France is saved
    forever.

        Archives parlementaires, XLVII, p 458

(c) The popular revolt

35 During this time [10 August 1792], the inhabitants of all the
    Fauxbourgs were repairing to the Palace and to the National
    Assembly, accompanied by all the Sections of Paris, armed in the
    same manner as they were on the 20th. of June, and calling for the
    dethronement of the King – that he was a Traitor and had forfeited
40 the Crown. . . . The Palace of the Tuileries is almost wholly
    destroyed, all the doors and windows of it being broken to
    pieces. . . . During all these disorders, the King and the Royal
    Family were sitting among the Deputies of the National Assembly
    where they had taken refuge. . . . The Sans-Culottes have now
45 obtained all their ends.

                    ★   ★   ★

        The people soon assembled in very great numbers in the Champ
    de Mars. The Municipal Officers on horseback, and in their scarves,
    proclaimed in every quarter of the town, that the country was in
    danger, and that it became all good citizens to fly to its relief. . . .
50 The mob proclaimed in answer to the Municipal Officers, that they
    had no objection to fly to the frontiers to beat the foreign enemy, and
    they wished no better sport, but first they would purge the nation of
    its internal enemies.

                    ★   ★   ★

In different prisons, churches and convents the mob amused themselves with the victims and formed a mock Tribunal. Some idea of these infamous proceedings may be collected from the following barbarities exercised on the old Cardinal de la Rochefaucauld. His hands and feet were tied together; and the mob ordered him to acknowledge that during his whole life he had never believed in God, but had been a hypocrite. He made no answer. The mob then said, if you believe in God, we give him, the Virgin Mary or her bastard John five minutes to release you; and so saying they cut him in pieces.

*　　*　　*

On the 20th. inst. the National Convention assembled for the first time. . . . The Convention instantly sent a deputation to the National Assembly, to announce its organisation, and that on that day or the ensuing one it would take possession of the Salle de Manage. . . . This is the second Legislature terminated, after having occasioned a second Revolution, not less fatal to the Constitution decreed by the first, than that Constitution had been to the Government which had ruled France for fourteen centuries.

The Times, 16 August, 8, 12 and 21 September 1792

(d) The elimination of the monarchy (1)

12 August 1792 – The Assembly, having first declared itself permanent, decreed, in the course of the day, that the executive power was withdrawn from the King, that his ministers had lost the confidence of the nation, and that, for the present, the government should be trusted to a ministry named by themselves; that the primary assemblies should be convened for the twenty-sixth of this month, to which all *citoyens* should be admitted without distinction of rank or property in order to appoint a national convention to meet at Paris on the twentieth of September to decide ultimately upon the forfeiture of the Crown and the mode of establishing an executive power; that His Most Christian Majesty should be lodged in some place of safety and that the civil list should no longer be continued.

Despatches of Earl Gower, p 208

(e) The elimination of the monarchy (2)

22 September 1792 – The Convention was going to adjourn for an hour or two when Mr. d'Herbois, one of the members for Paris, said there was a declaration they could not dispense making that night, which was the abolition of Royalty; this after a very short conversation was unanimously agreed to, and on Saturday the suppression of every attribute of Royalty wherever it might be, and the destruction of everything that recalled the idea of such a government was decreed; the seal was to be changed and to bear a

Roman fasces surmounted with a cap of Liberty and the exergue La République Française, and all public deeds were in future to be dated from the first year of the Republic.

Ibid, p 253

Questions

a What justification had Vergniaud for his criticism of Louis XVI in extract *a*?

b On what grounds was the king regarded as a 'tyrant' (line 14)?

c What does extract *c* suggest were the motives and passions behind the September Massacres?

★ d Can Louis XVI's dethronement be considered a triumph for the direct democracy of the Paris sections?

VII   The Convention and the Failure of the Girondins September 1792–June 1793

Introduction

In the autumn of 1792 the tide of war changed in favour of the French, and as long as victories were gained by their armies, the Girondins could remain in power. The trial and execution of the king, however, left them disunited and disorganised, and war with Britain and Spain was followed by French reverses in the Netherlands and elsewhere during the early months of 1793. There followed the rising of La Vendée and the desertion of the French commander, Charles François Dumouriez, who was a Girondin and constitutional monarchist. Their opponents demanded more energetic measures against the enemies of the Revolution. They had to agree to the setting up of the Revolutionary Tribunal and the Committee of Public Safety, but this did not save them. The Jacobins were ready to take advantage of their general unpopularity. At the end of May, a large crowd broke into the Convention and compelled it to send a number of leading Girondins to prison, whence they were sent by the Revolutionary Tribunal to execution:

1 The Girondins found it difficult to decide what should be done with Louis XVI for various reasons, but the Jacobins were united in wishing him to be brought to trial and punished. On the first day of the debate in the Convention, the youngest of its members, Antoine de Saint-Just, in a maiden speech, expressed the view that the king must die, not for what he had done, but for what he was, and other extracts in this section show the attitude taken by Thomas Paine and Robespierre.

2 The Convention decided in favour of a trial of the king, but one in which it should be both prosecutor and judge. The extract from the beginning of his interrogation shows how Louis refused to recognise the authority of the accusations made against him. His conviction of the high political crimes alleged against him was inevitable, and his defence by the young lawyer, Romain Desèze, was in vain. A view of the trial was expressed by Gouverneur Morris, the American Minister to France, whose personal sympathies were strongly monarchical. He mentioned the fatal evidence against Louis, the royal correspondence with Austria, discovered in the *armoire de fer*, the secret iron-box, at the Tuileries.

After his execution, France was seriously divided, effective government threatened and the coming of the Terror inevitable.

3 The war with Britain, which Brissot did not want, brought bad news, which caused rioting in Paris. This led Danton to make an impassioned speech to the Convention urging the formation of the Revolutionary Tribunal for the summary trial of traitors. This was established; and so was the Committee of Public Safety as the executive authority throughout the Republic, and the Convention appointed Danton and other Jacobins to this to indicate its mistrust of the Girondins. When Marat the next month issued a placard against Dumouriez and the Girondins, the Convention decided that he should be tried for libel by the Revolutionary Tribunal, which unanimously acquitted him.

4 The Jacobins were now in alliance with the Commune of Paris, the city's administrative body, and the sections, the meetings of the local constituency divisions in which the sans-culottes were powerful. In April the Commune named 22 leading Girondins as traitors, and the next month the sections compelled the Convention to introduce the control of corn prices. By now the Jacobins were ready to strike, and the Girondins fell from power, an event which Thibadeau regarded as the beginning of the Terror and the end of the effective power of the Convention.

1 The Debate about the King

(a) *The parties divided*

31 October 1792 – Whether the King ought or ought not to be judged is not merely considered as a matter of justice or even of expediency, but, most unfortunately, it has become a party question, in which passion may have more weight than either. Danton's party know
5 that the Girondists wish to save the King, which is reason sufficient with the former to do everything in their power to promote his trial and condemnation, and to represent the opposition of the other party as a proof of their being aristocrats and royalists in their hearts.

Marat, who is the great agent of Danton and Robespierre, declares
10 that it is highly unjust and would be a shameful deviation from the flattering tenet of égalité, after having condemned M. de la Porte and inferior criminals, to pass over the greatest criminal of all. Finally, I have been impressed with fears respecting the fate of the King from a variety of circumstances, too minute to be mentioned, which have
15 struck me very lately. It is certainly horrid and disgraceful to human nature, but I am afraid that the populace of this city [Paris] have heard so much of a grand example that ought to be exhibited to Europe, and their imaginations have dwelt so long on the idea of a King being tried for his life and afterwards led to execution, that they

cannot with patience bear the thoughts of being disappointed of such an extraordinary spectacle.

John Moore, *Journal During a Residence in France* (1793), p 61

(b) Speeches in the Convention: Saint-Just

13 November 1792 – A man of great spirit might say, in another age, that a king should be accused, not for the crimes of his administration, but for the crime of having been king, as that is an usurpation which nothing on earth can justify. With whatever illusions, whatever conventions, monarchy cloaks itself, it remains an eternal crime against which every man has the right to rise and to arm himself. Monarchy is an outrage which even the blindness of an entire people cannot justify; that people, by the example it gave, is guilty before nature, and all men hold from nature the secret mission to destroy such domination wherever it may be found.

No man can reign innocently. The folly is all too evident. Every king is a rebel and an usurper. Do kings themselves treat otherwise those who seek to usurp their authority? Was not Cromwell's memory brought to trial? And certainly Cromwell was no more usurper than Charles I, for when a people is so weak as to yield to the tyrant's yoke, domination is the right of the first comer and is no more sacred or legitimate for one than for any other. Those are considerations which a great and republican people ought not to forget when judging a king.

Regicide and Revolution, Speeches at the Trial of Louis XVI (ed. Michael Walzer and trans. Marian Rothstein, 1974), pp 124–5

(c) Speeches in the Convention: Thomas Paine

21 November 1792 – Louis XVI, considered as an individual, is an object beneath the notice of the Republic; but when he is looked upon as a part of that band of conspirators, as an accused man whose trial may lead all nations in the world to know and detest the disastrous system of monarchy and the plots and intrigues of their own courts, he ought to be tried.

If the crimes for which Louis XVI is arraigned were absolutely personal to him, without reference to general conspiracies and confined to the affairs of France, the plea of inviolability, the folly of the moment, might have been urged in his behalf with some appearance of reason; but he is arraigned not only for treasons against France, but for having conspired against all Europe, and if France is to be just to all Europe we ought to use every means in our power to discover the whole extent of that conspiracy. France is now a republic; she has completed her revolution; but she cannot earn all its advantages so long as she is surrounded with despotic governments. Their armies and their marine oblige her also to keep

troops and ships in readiness. It is therefore her immediate interest that all nations shall be as free as herself; that revolutions shall be
60 universal; and since the trial of Louis XVI can serve to prove to the world the flagitiousness of governments in general and the necessity of revolutions, she ought not to let slip so precious an opportunity.

The Writings of Thomas Paine (ed. M. D. Conway, 3 vols, 1894–5), III, p 117

(d) Speeches in the Convention: Robespierre

3 December 1792 – For myself I abhor the death penalty freely imposed by your laws, and I have neither love nor hatred for Louis; I
65 hate only crime. I demanded the abolition of the death penalty from the Assembly which you still call Constituent, and it is not my fault if the first principles of reason seemed to them moral and political heresies. But if you never thought to invoke them in favour of so many unhappy people whose crimes are less their own than those of
70 the government, by what fatal chance do you remember them now solely to plead the cause of the greatest of all criminals? You ask for an exception to the death penalty for him who alone could make it legitimate! Yes, the death penalty in general is a crime, and for this single reason that, according to the indestructible principles of
75 nature, it can only be justified in cases where it is necessary for safety of individuals or public order. Now, public safety never requires the death penalty against ordinary crimes, because society can always prevent them by other means and render the culprit incapable of doing further harm. But a King, dethroned in the midst of a
80 Revolution as yet unsupported by laws, a King whose very name draws the scourge of war on a nation in tumult, neither prison nor exile can make his existence indifferent to the public welfare; and this cruel exception to the ordinary laws which justice prescribes can be imputed only to the nature of his crimes. I pronounce with regret
85 this fatal truth – But Louis must die because the motherland must live.

Morse Stephens, op cit, II, pp 365–6

Questions

a From whom had the Parisians heard of 'a grand example that ought to to exhibited to Europe' (lines 17–18)?

b Compare the arguments put forward by Saint-Just, Paine and Robespierre in condemning Louis XVI.

c Why did Robespierre refer slightingly to the Constituent Assembly in extract *d* (line 66)?

★ d Why did the issue of the king's trial and execution present the Girondins with a serious political dilemma?

2   The King's Trial and Execution

(a) *The interrogation of the king, 11 December 1792*

The President. Louis, the French people accuse you of having committed a multitude of crimes to establish your tyranny by destroying its liberty. You have, on 20 June 1789, attacked the sovereignty of the people by suspending the assemblies of its representation and by expelling them while they were still sitting. The proof of this is in the report addressed to the Tennis Court at Versailles by the members of the Constituent Assembly. On 23 June you wished to dictate the Nation's laws, you surrounded its representatives by troops, you presented to them two royal declarations subversive to all freedom, and you ordered them to disperse. Your declarations and the Assembly's reports prove these crimes. What have you to say in reply?

Louis. There exists no law to impeach me.

The President. You despatched an army against the citizens of Paris. Your minions shed the blood of several of them, and you did not remove this army until the taking of the Bastille and the general rising showed you that the people were victorious. The interviews which you had on 9, 12 and 14 July with various deputations make it clear that these were your intentions, and the massacres of the Tuileries testify against you. What have you to say in reply?

Louis. I was the master empowered to despatch troops at that time and to shed blood.

Procès-Verbal *(Convention nationale)*, IV, p 178

(b) *Romain Desèze's defence of Louis, 26 December 1792*

Louis mounted the throne at the age of twenty; and even then he set the example of morality; he was governed by no culpable weakness, no corrupting passion; he was economical, just and severe and proved himself the friend of his country. The nation desired the abolition of a crushing tax; he revoked it. The people demanded the abolition of servitude; he abolished it in his domains. They prayed for reforms in the criminal law; he made these reforms. They demanded that thousands of Frenchmen whom the rigour of our usages had excluded from political rights should acquire and enjoy them; he conceded them. The people demanded liberty; he gave it. He even anticipated their wishes by his sacrifices; and yet it is in the name of this same people that men now demand – Citizens, I do not propose to continue – I pause before the tribunal of history. Remember that it will judge your decision, and your decision will be the voice of ages.

Gerald A. Tate, *Louis XVI, The Last Phase* (1929), p 28

(c) An American view

To Thomas Jefferson, 21 December 1792 – I come now to the trial of the
King and the circumstances connected therewith. To a person less
40 intimately acquainted than you are with the history of human affairs,
it would seem strange that the mildest monarch who ever filled the
French throne, one who is precipitated from it precisely because he
would not adopt the harsh measures of his predecessors, a man who
none can charge with a criminal or cruel act, should be persecuted as
45 one of the most defarious tyrants that ever disgraced the annals of
human nature. That he, Louis the sixteenth, should be prosecuted
even to the death. Yet such is the fact. I think it is highly probable
that he may suffer, and that for the following causes. The majority of
the Assembly find it necessary to raise, against this unhappy Prince,
50 the national odium, in order to justify the dethroning him (which
after what he had suffered appeared to be necessary even to their
safety) and to induce the ready adoption of the republican form of
government. Being in possession of his papers and those of his
servants, it was easy (if they would permit themselves to extract, to
55 comment, to suppress and to mutilate), it was *very* easy to create
such opinions as they might think proper. The rage, which has been
excited, was terrible, and although it begins to subside, the
Convention are still in great streights; fearing to acquit, fearing to
condemn, and yet urged to destroy their captive Monarch. The
60 violent part are clamorous against him. . . . The monarchic and
aristocratic parties wish his death, in the belief that such a catastrophe
would shock the national feelings, awaken their hereditary
attachments and turn into the channels of loyalty the impetuous tide
of opinion. Thus he has become the common object of hatred to all
65 parties, because he has never been the decided patron of any one.

*A Diary of the French Revolution by Gouverneur Morris 1756–
1816* (ed. Beatrice Cary Davenport, 2 vols, 1972), II, p 581

(d) The execution of the king, 21 January 1793

Citizens, the tyrant is no more. For a long time the cries of his
victims, who war and domestic dissensions have spread over France
and Europe, loudly protested his existence. He has paid the penalty,
and only acclamations for the Republic and for liberty have been
70 heard from the peoples. . . . The National Convention and the
French people must now have only one mind, only one sentiment,
that of liberty and civic fraternity.

Now, above all, we need peace within the Republic and the most
active watch upon the enemies of liberty amongst us. Never could
75 circumstances demand more urgently from all citizens the sacrifice
of their own passions and opinions concerning the act of national

justice which has been executed. To-day the French people can have
no other passion than that for liberty.

Procès-Verbal (Convention nationale), V, p 474

(e) A British view

Posterity, in condemning these infamous judges who have sacrificed
Louis to the fury and ambition of the vilest of men, will extend their
censures yet further; and in the warmth of virtuous indignation, will
not refrain from blasting the memory of that minister [Necker], who
to gratify a selfish vanity, directed the royal victim to make a first
step towards that precipice, from the brink of which he is now
precipitated.

Posterity will condemn those members of the Constituent
Assembly, who allured by the metaphor of false philosophy, madly
burst asunder the bonds of popular subordination; tore down the
pillars of monarchy and religion, and left Louis defenceless, forsaken
and abandoned to those hordes of Monsters, who, under the
different appellation of Legislative Assemblies, Clubs and Sections,
have inflicted upon their miserable victim a thousand agonising
deaths and apprehensions before they delivered him up to the axe of
the executioner.

The Times, 25 January 1793

Questions

a Do extracts *a*, *b* and *c* support the view that the condemnation of
Louis XVI by the Convention was itself a crime?

b Does extract *c* suggest the reason for the call for national unity in
extract *d*?

c What was the act of 'selfish vanity' for which Necker was
condemned in extract *e* (line 83)?

d 'At home this killing of a King has divided all friends, and abroad
it has united all enemies' (Thomas Carlyle). Discuss this
assertion.

3   War and Rebellion

(a) War with England

Jean-Pierre Brissot to Francisco Miranda, 10 January 1793 – The war
with England attracts all our concern and absorbs all our attention.
Everything seems to make it certain; however, when one considers
that fundamentally there is no reasonable motive, and that when also
one sees the immense wealth gained by this nation while we wage
war, one is completely surprised by this folly of the cabinet of St.

James. Whatever may be its intention, we have to face and prepare for it.

> J. P. Brissot, *Correspondance et Papiers* (ed. C. Perroud, 1912), p 335

(b) Danton: on the Revolutionary Tribunal

10 March 1793 – I demand that the Revolutionary Tribunal be set up during this present sitting and that the executive power, in the new organization, receive the necessary means of action and power. I do not ask that anything be upset; I only suggest ways of improvement.

I demand that the Convention considers my arguments and ignores the harmful and disgraceful slanders which people have dared to make about me. I demand that as soon as the measures for general security have been taken, your commissioners immediately leave without any objections from anyone wherever he sits in this chamber – that they disperse into the departments, that they there arouse the citizens and restore their love of liberty, and even if they regret not passing useful decrees or opposing harmful ones, they will remember that their absence has saved the country.

> Morse Stephens, op cit, II, p 197

(c) The decree concerning the rebellion, 19 March 1793

1. Those who are or will be accused of having taken part in revolts or counter-revolutionary risings, which have broken out or will break out during the period of recruitment in the various departments of the Republic, and those who assume or will assume the white cockade or any other sign of rebellion, are beyond the law. Consequently, they cannot benefit from the provisions of the laws concerning criminal procedure and the institution of juries.

2. If they are taken or arrested carrying arms, they shall, within twenty-four hours, be delivered to the executor of criminal judgements and put to death after the sentence has been approved and upheld by a military commission formed by the officers of each division employed against the rebels. . . .

6. Priests, former nobility and gentry, the agents and servants of all these people, foreigners, those who were employed or exercised any public function in the former government or since the revolution, those who have encouraged or supported any rebels, leaders, instigators, those who held any rank in the rebellious groups, and those who shall be convicted of murder, arson or pillage, will undergo the punishment of death.

> *Procès-Verbal (Convention nationale)*, VIII, p 88

(d) The Committee of Public Safety, 6 April 1793

1. There will be formed, by open vote, a committee of public safety, composed of nine members of the National Convention.

2. This committee will deliberate in secret; it will be expected to supervise and accelerate the operation of the administrative duties entrusted to the provisional executive council, including the power even to suspend its decrees if it believes them contrary to the national interest, providing that it informs the Convention without delay.

3. It is authorized to take, in urgent circumstances, measures for the general exterior and interior defence; and its decisions, signed by the majority of its deliberating members, which shall not be less than two-thirds, shall be executed without delay by the provisional executive council; it shall in any case only issue warrants of search or arrest, if they are not in accordance with this manner of execution, on condition that it is immediately reported to the Convention.

E. Reich, *Select Documents Illustrating Medieval and Modern History* (1905), pp 437–8

(e) Marat: on the treason of Dumouriez

12 April 1793 – Friends, we are betrayed! To arms! to arms! This is the terrible hour when the defenders of the motherland must conquer or be enslaved beneath the ruins of the country. Frenchmen, never has your liberty been in greater peril; the base treachery of our enemies has at last reached its climax, and to complete it, Dumouriez, their accomplice, is marching on Paris. The manifest treason of the general allied to him leaves no doubt that this plan of rebellion and shameful audaciousness was directed by the criminal faction which he has maintained and glorified, such as La Fayette, and that he has deceived us about his conduct until the moment of decision . . . . But, brothers and friends, these are not your only dangers; you must be convinced of an even sadder fact; your greatest enemies are among you; they direct your operations and reprisals, they control your means of defence! Yes, brothers and friends, it is in the senate that parricidal hands tear at your hearts! Yes, the counter-revolution is in the government and the National Convention; it is there in the centre of your safety and your hopes that the criminal delegates hold the threads of the plot which they have woven with the band of despots who approach to slaughter us! There is a cabal directed by the English and other courts . . . . But already your courage and loyalty are aroused by your indignation. Come, republicans, let us arm ourselves!

Adresse des Amis de la Liberté à leurs Frères des Départements, Morse Stephens, op cit, I, p 446

Questions

a What does extract *a* suggest was Brissot's attitude towards the likelihood of war with Britain?

b How does extract *c* indicate what had provoked the revolt against the Republic?

c What is the meaning of the reference to 'Dumouriez' in extract *e* (line 60)?

★ d To what extent were the principal instruments of the Terror created in the spring of 1793?

4 The Fall of the Girondins

(a) The sans-culottes

What is a sans-culotte? A sans-culotte is a man who goes everywhere on his own two feet, who has none of the millions you are all after, no mansion, no lackeys to wait on him, and who lives simply with his wife and children, if he has any, on the fourth or fifth
5 storey. He is useful because he knows how to plough a field, to handle a forge, a saw and a file, to cover a roof, to make a pair of shoes, and to shed the last drop of his blood to save the Republic. And since he works, you are sure not to find him at the Café de Chartres [frequented by Orleanists] . . . . In the evening, he goes to
10 the meeting of his Section, not powdered and perfumed and dressed up in the hope of being noticed by all the citizenesses in the spectators' galleries, but in order to support the right sort of resolutions with all his power and to smash the vile faction of useless time-servers.
15 For the rest, a sans-culotte has always his sharp sabre ready to cut off the ears of the malevolent. Sometimes he marches with his pike. But at the first sound of the drum, he can be seen leaving for the Vendée, for the Army of the Alps or for the Army of the North.

Jean-Baptiste Vintergnier in A. Soboul, 'Problèmes du Travail en l'an II,' *Journal de Psychologie* (1955), pp 39–58

(b) A sans-culottes paternoster

Our Father, who are in Heaven, from whence you protect in such an
20 admirable manner the French Republic and the Sans-Culottes, your most ardent defenders; may your name be blessed and sanctified among us, as it always has been; may your steadfast will, making men live free, equal and happy, be done on Earth as it is in Heaven. Give us to-day the daily bread which we eat despite the vain efforts
25 of Pitt, Coburg and all the Tyrants united to keep us hungry. Forgive us the faults which we have committed, in supporting for so long the Tyrants from which we have purged France, as we forgive the Enslaved Nations, when they imitate us. Do not suffer them any

longer to endure the fetters which restrain them and from which they are strenuously seeking to free themselves; but may they deliver themselves, as we have done, from Nobles, Priests and Kings. So be it.

Annales historiques de la Révolution française (1924), p 69

(c) An address by the Commune of Paris to the Convention

15 April 1793 – We here recognize solemnly that the majority of the Convention is guiltless, because it has struck down the tyrant. We do not ask for the panic-stricken dissolution of the Convention or the suspension of the machinery of government; far from us this truly anarchic idea, imagined by traitors who, to strengthen themselves against this demand which will drive them from the chamber, wish at least to exploit the confusion and distress in France; we come, fortified by that part of public opinion represented by the majority of the sections, to arouse the cry of vengeance which will be repeated throughout the whole of France. . . .

The general assembly of the sections of Paris, having thoroughly discussed the conduct of the deputies of the Convention, has decided that those contained in the list below have, according to its most considered opinion, openly violated the trust of their constituents.

Brissot, Gaudet, Vergniaud, Gensonné, Grangeneuve, Buzot, Barbaroux, Salles, Biroteau, Pontécoulant, Pétron, Lanjuinais, Valzé, Hardy, Lehardy, Jean-Baptiste Louvet, Gorsas, Fauchet, Lanthenas, Lasource, Valady, Chambon.

Procès-Verbal (Convention nationale), IX, p 273

(d) The First Law of the Maximum, 4 May 1793

1. Immediately after the publication of this decree, every merchant, farmer or landowner concerned with corn and flour shall be required to make to the municipality of the place of their residence a declaration of the quantity and nature of corn or flour which they possess and approximately how much corn remains with them to be threshed. The district directories shall appoint commissioners to implement the execution of this measure in the various municipalities. . . .

3. The municipalities shall send without delay to the directory of their district a table of declared and verified prices for corn and flour; the district directories shall pass without delay the result to the directory of their department, which shall draw up from them a general list and transmit it to the Minister of the Interior and the National Convention.

Ibid, XI, p 41

(e) The arrest of the Girondins, 2 June 1793

65 Anyone who spoke of order was dishonoured as a royalist; anyone
who spoke of laws was ridiculed as a *statesman*, an honourable name
which became harmful and a reason for proscription. It began with
mutual abuse and accusations and ended with proscriptions. The
Gironde was the final limit between light and darkness. When it was
70 overthrown, we fell into chaos. . . .

   As people seek in ordinary times to raise themselves, so they
strove in this time of calamity to abase themselves to be forgotten or
degrade themselves to secure forgiveness for their superiority. They
hid not only their birth and wealth, but all the more legitimate
75 advantages offered by nature or education. Everyone belittled
themselves to pass below the popular level. People abandoned
costume, manners, elegance, neatness, conveniences of life,
politeness and propriety so as not to excite the envy of those to
whom all this was unknown.

80   The National Convention itself was only a nominal assembly, a
passive instrument of the Terror. Upon the ruins of its independence
rose that monstrous dictatorship which became so well-known
under the name of the Committee of Public Safety. The Terror
isolated and stupified the deputies as it did the ordinary citizens. On
85 entering the Assembly, the mistrustful members watched their
words and actions, fearful that they might be made a crime. In fact,
everything mattered – the place where they sat, a gesture, a look, a
murmur, a smile. Everyone flocked to the summit of the Mountain,
which passed for the highest degree of republicanism; the right wing
90 was deserted after the Girondins had been wrested from it; those
who had sat there with them and had too much conscience or shame
to become Montagnards took refuge in the Plain, which was always
ready to receive men who sought safety in its complaisance or
anonymity. . . .

> Antoine-Claire Thibadeau, *Mémoires sur la Convention et le
> Directoire* (2 vols, 1824), I, pp 36 and 46

Questions

a On what grounds did the sans-culottes claim the moral
   leadership of the Revolution?

b What circumstances led to the passing of the maximum of corn
   prices?

c Explain the references to 'the Mountain' and 'the Plain' in
   extract *e* (lines 88 and 92).

★ *d* Do you agree that the Girondins were 'law-abiding and tolerant,
   but also incompetent, irresponsible and inflexible'?

VIII   The Committee of Public Safety June 1793–August 1795

Introduction

Mindful that the Convention had been elected to produce a new constitution, the Jacobins drew up one that was extremely democratic. It included universal manhood suffrage and plebiscites on important questions, but it did not meet the economic demands of the enragés (wild men) and was suspended until the end of the war. The period from the autumn of 1793 to the summer of 1794 saw the organisation of the Terror and the rise and fall of Robespierre. The murder of Marat strengthened Robespierre, and by March 1794 he was able to triumph over the enragés and Dantonists. There followed four months of dictatorship by Robespierre and the Committee of Public Safety, which was strengthened by the Law of Prairial. A 'reign of virtue' was established with its own religious 'Cult of the Supreme Being'. But the existence of the Terror was threatened by the victories of the French armies and economic discontent. It came to an end with the overthrow of the Robespierrists on 9 Thermidor (27 July 1794); and the nature of the reaction was shown by the promulgation of the Constitution of the Year III the next year:

1 The Constitution of 1793 sought to express the ideal of direct democracy of the ancient Greeks and Rousseau, which held that people cannot be represented. The extract from Jacques Roux's protest shows that the enragés and sans-culottes now wanted economic equality instead of the mere equality before the law hitherto sought by the revolutionaries. The Committee's response to this was to pass a decree against hoarding, which was so severe that it could hardly be enforced. Robespierre came on to the Committee in July 1793, when he wrote a series of notes (published after his death as a catechism) expressing the programme he wished the Jacobins to follow to achieve his ideal republic of liberty and virtue.

2 By now the situation of the Committee seemed desperate. France was at war against most of Europe, and there was widespread revolt in the provinces. The Terror came in with the levée en masse and the emergency, discretionary government of the Declaration of 10 October 1793, and it was enforced by the representatives sent out on mission by the Committee.

3 Robespierre read his speech of 5 February 1794 in the name of the Committee of Public Safety. In it he expressed his conception of the principles underlying democratic government, which were the aim of the regime now fighting for its life. The remaining extracts in this section form a discussion of the two developing threats to the Terror – triumph in war and the hardship still suffered by the people of Paris. The last extract, from a speech by a speaker prominent in the Jacobin Club of Paris, shows the emotional atmosphere of the time.

4 The Law of 22 Prairial has been said to inaugurate a period known as the Great Terror. Its introduction by one of Robespierre's closest associates explains how the terrorists viewed the situation. The fear caused by the executions which followed contributed, however, to the end of the Terror. Robespierre's defiant last speech could not save him. The last two extracts offer explanations of both his rise and his fall from power.

5 The men who overthrew Robespierre were largely inspired by self-preservation. To gain popularity, they abolished the Committee of Public Safety, the Revolutionary Tribunal and other aspects of the 'revolutionary government', and they distanced themselves in various ways from Robespierre and the Terror. Moreover, they changed the course of the Revolution. The Constitution of 1795 sought to establish the supremacy of property by limiting the vote to taxpayers and reverting to a system of indirect election.

1 The Jacobin Regime

(a) The Constitution of 1793

2. The French people is divided, for the exercise of its sovereignty, into primary assemblies of the Cantons.

7. The sovereign people is the entire body of French citizens.

8. It nominates its deputies directly.

5   9. It delegates to electors the choice of officials, public assessors and appeal judges.

10. It deliberates on laws.

11. The primary assemblies consist of the citizens domiciled for six months in each Canton.

10   12. They comprise not less than 200 and not more than 600 citizens called upon to vote.

16. Elections are conducted by ballot or word of mouth as each voter chooses.

19. Votes on laws are expressed as 'yes' or 'no'.

15   32. The French people assemble every year on 1 May for elections.

34. An extraordinary meeting of a primary assembly meets at the request of a fifth of the citizens who have the right to vote.

36. The extraordinary assemblies only deliberate if over a half of the citizens with the right to vote are present.

37. The citizens in a primary assembly nominate an elector for every 200 citizens, whether present or not. . . .

40. The session of the legislative body is for one year.

41. It meets on 1 July.

53. The legislative body proposes laws and passes decrees.

56. The projected law is printed and sent to all the Communes of the Republic under this title: Proposed Law.

59. If, forty days after sending out the proposed law, a tenth of the primary assemblies in each of a majority of the Departments has not objected, the project is accepted and becomes law.

60. If there is an objection, the legislative body convokes the primary assemblies.

Buchez and Roux, op cit, XXXI, pp 400–14

(b) Rousseau on sovereignty (1758)

It is not enough for the assembled people to have once fixed the constitution of the State by giving its sanction to a body of law; it is not enough for it to have set up a perpetual government or provided once for all for the election of magistrates. Besides the extraordinary assemblies unforeseen circumstances may demand, there must be fixed periodical assemblies which cannot be abrogated or prorogued, so that on the proper day the people is legitimately called together by law without need of any formal summoning. . . .

The greater or less frequency with which lawful assemblies occur depends on so many considerations that no exact rules about them can be given. It can only be said generally that the stronger the government, the more often should the sovereign show itself.

The Social Contract and Discourses by Jean-Jacques Rousseau, p 80

(c) A protest to the Convention by Jacques Roux

25 June 1793 – The Constitutional Act is going to be presented to the sovereign for ratification. Does it proscribe speculation? No. Have you pronounced the death penalty for hoarders? No. Have you set limits to freedom of trade? No. . . . We are telling you that you have not yet done everything possible for the happiness of the people. Liberty is nothing but a vain illusion when one class of men can starve another and go unpunished. Equality is nothing but a vain illusion when the rich, because of their monopoly, exercise the right of life and death over their fellow-men. The Republic is nothing but a vain illusion when from day to day the counter-revolution manipulates the price of food which three-quarters of the citizens cannot reach without shedding tears. Make another pronouncement then. The sans-culottes will exercise your decrees with their pikes.

Richard Bienvenue, *The Ninth of Thermidor: The Fall of Robespierre* (1968), pp 18–19

(d) The decree on hoarding, 26 July 1793

The National Convention, considering all the ills that hoarders inflict on society by their murderous speculations on the most
60   pressing needs of life and on public poverty, decree the following:

    1. Hoarding is a capital crime.

    2. Those are declared guilty of hoarding who remove from circulation the most-needed commodities or foodstuffs, which they divert and retain stored in some place without offering them for sale
65   daily and openly.

    3. They are equally declared hoarders who destroy or willingly allow to perish the most-needed foodstuffs and commodities.

    4. The most-needed commodities are bread, meat, wine, corn, flour, vegetables, fruit, butter, vinegar, cider, brandy, charcoal,
70   tallow, wood, oil, soda, soap, dried, smoked, salted or pickled meat and fish, honey, sugar, paper, hemp, war or spun wool, leather, iron and steel, copper, clothes, napkins and generally all woven textiles, including the materials from which they are made, with the exception of silk.

Procès-Verbal (Convention nationale), XVII, p 274

(e) Robespierre's catechism, July 1793

75   What is our aim?

It is the use of the Constitution for the benefit of the people.

Who are likely to oppose us?

The rich and corrupt.

What methods will they employ?
80   Slander and hypocrisy.

What factors will encourage the use of such means?

The ignorance of the sans-culottes.

The people must therefore be instructed.

What obstacles are there to its enlightenment?
85   The paid journalists, who mislead it every day by shameless impostures.

What conclusion follows?

That we ought to proscribe those writers as the most dangerous enemies of the country and to circulate an abundance of good
90   literature.

What other obstacle is there to the instruction of the people?

Its poverty.

When, then, will the people be educated?

When it has enough bread to eat, and when the rich and the

Government cease bribing treacherous pens and tongues to deceive it; when their interests are identified with those of the people.

When will this be?

Never.

What other obstacles are there to the achievement of freedom?

The war at home and abroad.

By what means can the foreign war be ended?

By placing republican generals at the head of our armies, and by punishing those who have betrayed us.

How can we end the civil war?

By punishing traitors and conspirators, especially those deputies and administrators who are to blame; by sending patriot troops under patriot leaders to reduce the aristocrats of Lyon, Marseille, Toulon, the Vendée, the Jura, and all other districts where the banner of royalism and rebellion has been raised; and by making a terrible example of all the criminals who have outraged liberty, and spilt the blood of patriots.

> J. M. Thompson, *Robespierre and the French Revolution* (1952), pp 79–80

Questions

a How did the Constitution of 1793 attempt to express Rousseau's ideal of direct democracy?

b In what sense is the word 'sovereign' used in lines 44 and 46?

c Does Robespierre's political programme in extract *e* suggest that he was 'before his time'?

d 'The grievances of the poor were due to economic problems which the Jacobins did not understand and could not cure' (J. M. Thompson). Discuss this statement.

2 The Terror

(a) *A member of the Convention on the Terror*

The Terror, as it is understood in France, subjected the whole nation to its bloody sceptre. It began on 31 May [1793] and ended on 9 Thermidor [27 July 1794]. . . . In a despotic state, the rulers, the courtiers and certain classes and individuals are at least unaffected by the terror they inspire. They are like gods who hurl thunderbolts without fear of being struck. In France under the reign of terror, no one was exempt; it hovered over everyone's head, striking them down indiscriminately; it was as arbitrary and swift as Death's scythe. The Convention, as well as the people, supplied its own contingent. Danton, Camille Desmoulins and the officers of the commune of Paris perished on the same scaffold to which they had dragged the Gironde. The people impartially applauded the death

of both executioners and victims. Marat, who seemed to be
unsurpassable in ferocity and whose execrable features so horribly
15 symbolized the terror, would not have escaped had not the dagger of
a courageous woman led him to the Pantheon. And Robespierre
finally, the high priest of the bloody fury, was reserved as its last
victim.

   A–C. Thibaudeau, op cit, I, p 44

(b) The assassination of Marat, 13 July 1793

Couthon complained [in the Convention] that the project of so
20 many crimes, discovered by the flight of the conspirators from
among the members of the Convention, should yet be
unpunished. . . .
   He moved,
   First, 'That the Revolutionary Tribunal should hasten the
25 judgment against the assassin of Marat; that it should immediately
proceed to the trial of Brissot, and prosecute as outlaws those
deputies, who, by their flight, had deprived themselves *of the
protection of the laws;*'
   Secondly, 'That a Decree of Accusation be passed against
30 Duperret, previously convicted of being an accomplice in the above
murder. . . .'

   The Times, 23 July 1793

(c) Levée en masse, 23 August 1793

The National Convention, having heard the report of its Committee
of Public Safety, decrees:
   1. From this time until the enemy is driven from the territory of
35 the Republic all Frenchmen are permanently sequestered for military
service.
   Young men will go to war, married men manufacture arms and
transport supplies, women make tents and uniforms and serve in
hospitals, children turn rags into bandages, and old people gather in
40 public places to stimulate the courage of the soldiers, the hatred of
kings and the unity of the Republic.
   2. National residences will be made into barracks and public
buildings into arms factories, and the soil of cellars be scoured to
extract saltpetre.
45 7. No one shall procure a substitute for any service to which he is
conscripted. Public officials shall remain at their posts.
   8. The levy will be general. Those citizens, who are unmarried or
childless widowers, from eighteen to fifty-five years old, will be the
first to go. They will assemble in the capital of their district, where
50 they will exercise themselves every day in the use of arms until
ordered to depart.

   Procès-Verbal (Convention nationale), XIX, p 188

(d) The Declaration of Revolutionary Government, 10 October 1793

The National Convention, having heard the report of its Committee of Public Safety, decrees:

1. The provisional government of France will be revolutionary until the coming of peace.

2. The Provisional Executive Council, ministers, generals and constituted authorities are placed under the supervision of the Committee of Public Safety, which will report weekly to the Convention.

3. All security measures should be taken by the Provisional Executive Council, upon the authorization of the Committee, which will report to the Convention.

5. Military commanders will be appointed by the National Convention upon the initiative of the Committee of Public Safety.

6. Since the inertia of the government has caused our reverses, time-limits will be fixed for the execution of laws and measures of public safety. Disregard of these limits will be punished as an attack on liberty.

P. Mautouchet (ed.), *Le Gouvernement révolutionnaire 10 août–4 brumaire an IV* (1912), p 196

(e) Letters from representatives on mission

Julien to Robespierre, Vannes, 22 October 1793 – The Vendée is destroyed, the rebels dispersed and the leaders either killed in battle or dead by suicide. There are a few priests left in the countryside, but we have the republicans on their heels, and fanaticism will repent of federalism.

★   ★   ★

Dumont to his Colleagues, 22 October 1793 – I have just brought about the arrest of some priests who took it upon themselves to celebrate holy days and Sundays. I am taking away the crucifixes and crosses, and soon I shall include in the proscription those black animals called priests. Yesterday, the 10th., I dissolved the Popular Society and named a secret committee to purify the list: this enactment was roundly applauded. I have likewise had it decreed that all drunkards and promoters of drunkenness be put into the lock-up. This will keep idleness and drunkenness from perverting the public welfare, and from depriving the defenders of the country of the brandy and beverages which are of the first necessity.

★   ★   ★

Callot-d'Herbois to Duplay, Commune Affranchie [Lyon], 15th.

Frumaire, Year II of the Republic [5 December 1793] – We have created a
commission which judges traitors as promptly as would a true
republican conscience. Sixty-four conspirators were shot yesterday
at the very place where they fired upon the patriots. Two hundred
90   and thirty will fall to-day in the execrable redoubts that belched forth
death upon the republic army. Such examples will influence the
cities that waver.

★   ★   ★

*Fréron to Moïse Bayle, Toulon, 6th. Nivôse, Year II of the Republic [26
December 1793]* – All goes well here: we have requisitioned twelve
95   thousand masons from the neighbouring departments to demolish
and raze the city. Since we made our entrance, we have caused two
hundred heads a day to fall.

E. L. Higgins, *The French Revolution as told by Contemporaries*
(1938), pp 323–7 passim

Questions

a   What were the political consequences of the assassination of
Marat?

b   What new development in warfare was introduced by the *levée en
masse?*

c   Does extract *d* suggest that the enforcement of the Terror in the
provinces depended upon the inclinations of the representatives
on mission?

★   *d*   Was the Terror essentially a defensive measure designed to
protect France and the Revolution?

3   The Virtuous Republic

(a) New ideals

We desire an order of things where all base and cruel passions are
enchained by the laws, all beneficent and general feelings awakened
by them; where ambition is the desire to serve glory and to be useful
to one's country; where distinctions arise only from equality itself;
5   where the citizen is subject to the magistrate, the magistrate to the
people, the people to justice; where the country secures the welfare
of each individual, and each individual proudly enjoys the prosperity
and glory of this country; where all minds are enlarged by the
constant interchange of republican sentiments and by the need of
10   earning the respect of a great people; where industry is an adornment
to the liberty that ennobles, and commerce is the source of public
wealth, not simply of monstrous riches for a few families.

We wish to substitute in our country morality for egotism,

probity for mere sense of honour, principle for habit, duty for etiquette, the rule of reason for the tyranny of custom, contempt for vice for contempt for misfortune, pride for insolence, large-mindedness for vanity, the love of glory for the love of money, good men for good company, merit for intrigue, talent for conceit, truth for show, the charm of happiness for the tedium of pleasure, the grandeur of man for the triviality of grand society, a people magnanimous, powerful and happy for a people lovable, frivolous and wretched – that is to say, all the virtues and miracles of the Republic for all the vices and puerilities of the monarchy.

> Maximilien Robespierre, *Report on the Principles of Public Morality*, 5 February 1794 in M. J. Sydenham, *The French Revolution* (1965), pp 207–8

(b) The Maximum: report by Bertrand Barère

22 February 1794 – Let us suspend our enjoyment of those pleasures of the table allowed to republicans and abandon those delicacies only for Sybarites so that citizens will purchase only what is necessary. Then, in a few months, free France will bless its defenders, and at the same time you will have founded republican principles, those of temperance and equality.

You will have done yet more; you will have changed the principles of French commerce. We have a monarchical commerce; it only seeks wealth; it has no patriotism; monarchies have no need of virtues. We must have a republican commerce, that is to say a commerce that loves its country above all else; a commerce with moderate profits and with virtues; republics have no other firm foundations.

> Morse Stephens, op cit, II, p 60

(c) The Maximum: report by an agent of the Ministry of the Interior

25 March 1794 – The first poster on the maximum, awaited impatiently, was put up [in Paris] during the afternoon and attracted everyone's attention. No one reading it failed to say that this maximum was very advantageous for the country people and the merchants. The article on meat prices was especially commented upon. Many people said that the maximum had been set at sixteen to eighteen sols in order to prevent sans–culottes from eating meat. It was observed that if the object of the law was to diminish the amount consumed, it would be better to fix the quantity that each family could have per décade or establish supplementary prices like those for bread. Only the rich would then bear the cost of the rise in price.

> Richard Bienvenue, op cit, p 86

(d) The lesson of victory

There, then, is the welcome result of your constancy, energy and unity. There are the fruits ripened by the light of the Revolution and preserved by the vigilance of the government which you have established and sustained by your confidence.

But if ever a reverse happens, if ever victory, does not remain constant, who must be held responsible and blamed for those national set-backs? Is it those who care ceaselessly for the Republic and the improvement of the people's lot? Or would it be more just and courageous to accuse only those men who set out ceaselessly to corrupt public opinion, undermine the hopes of all the citizens, frustrate the victories of our brave armies, mock the achievements of the Revolution and attack the government, being determined to weaken confidence in it, decry its policies or discourage its members when they cannot overwhelm them?

Bertrand Barère, *Report on the Capture of Charleroi to the Convention*, 27 June 1794, Morse Stephens, op cit, II, pp 73–4

(e) Exaltation and fear

It was not yesterday, citizens, that we knew that assassinations had been planned by the tyrants; it was not yesterday that we knew that the inventiveness of tyrants was limited to criminal deeds. We knew that the execrable Pitt subsidized all of the crimes. We knew that he was obstinately going ahead with the plan to dissolve the National Convention by multiplied murders. We knew that in this majestic Convention, whose courage and ceaselessly energetic efforts oppressed and tormented him for the sole reason that the labours of the Convention ensured the happiness of all men enjoying liberty; we knew, I say, that in the midst of this representative body of a free, strong and powerful people, there was not one friend of virtue whose head had not been proscribed by these odious English and Austrian ministers, the slaves of tyrants.

Jean Collot d'Herbois, *Speech at the Jacobin Club, 6 Prairial, Year II* 25 May 1714, R. T. Bienvenue, op cit, p 95

Questions

a Is Robespierre's comparison between the monarchy and the republic in extract *a* a caricature or does it represent their essential difference?

b Does extract *c* suggest that the Parisians shared Barère's idealistic view of the Maximum in extract *b*?

c How did Barère and d'Herbois in extracts *d* and *e* seek to show that France needed the Terror in both triumph and adversity?

★ d 'He will go far because he believes everything he says' (Mirabeau). Discuss this estimate of Robespierre.

4 The Fall of Robespierre

(a) The Law of 22 Prairial (10 June 1794)

The period necessary for punishing the fatherland's enemies shall be only the time it takes to recognize them. It is a matter less of punishing them than of annihilating them.

A revolution like ours is nothing but a rapid succession of conspiracies because it is a war of tyranny against liberty. It is not a question of making a few examples, but of exterminating the implacable satellites of tyranny or of perishing with the Republic. Indulgence towards them is atrocious, clemency is parricide. . . .

The Republic, attacked in its infancy by enemies as perfidious as they are numerous, must strike them with the speed of lightning while taking the precautions necessary for saving slandered patriots.

Georges Auguste Couthon in the Convention, ibid, p 98

(b) A summary of Robespierre's last speech

Robespierre, who for a long time had not appeared in the assembly [i.e. the Convention], mounted the platform and spoke.

He read a long speech in which he began by extolling his virtue. He complained of being slandered and indicated as enemies of the people all those who appeared to him to be opposed to his projects. He next decried, in a long diatribe, all the operations of the government; he declaimed successively against the Committees of Public Safety, of General Security and of Finance. Without formally complaining of the political opposition offered by this last committee to his projects to take over the finances, he tried to include it in the condemnation by accusing it of acting in a counter-revolutionary way towards the finances of the republic.

He then stated that the patriots were oppressed. 'Why,' he said, 'has this account of the success of the armies been given to you? Dumouriez's system is followed in Belgium; lifeless trees of liberty are planted, the gunners of Paris are taken away, a camp is formed which could become dangerous, etc.'

He added that there was a wish to change the situation of the republic; and finally he announced that he would put forward the only measures to save the republic.

Moniteur, XXI (11 Thermidor, Year II–29 July 1794), p 329

(c) The end of Robespierre and the Maximum

In two days after the execution of Robespierre, the whole commune of Paris, consisting of about sixty persons, were guillotined in less than an hour and a half in the Place de la Révolution; and though I was standing above a hundred paces from the place of execution, the blood of the victims streamed under my feet. What surprised me was, as each head fell into the basket, the cry of the people was no

other than a repetition of '*A bas le Maximum!*' which was caused by
the privations imposed on the populace by the rigorous exaction of
40 that law which set certain prices upon all sorts of provisions, and
which was attributed to Robespierre. The persons who now suffered
were all of different trades; and, many of them, indeed, had taken
advantage of that law and had abused it by forcing the farmers and
others, who supplied the Paris market, to sell at the maximum price,
45 and they retailed at an enormous advance to those who could afford
to pay. I did not see Robespierre going to the guillotine, but I have
been informed that the crowd, which attended the waggon in which
he passed on that occasion, went so far as to thrust their umbrellas
into the waggon against his body.

Archibald Hamilton Rowan, *Autobiography* (ed. W. H.
Drummond, 1840), p 135

(d) A terrorist's defence

50 Let us ask, as already has been done, why we allowed Robespierre to
go so far. Not one single fact has been established, nor one single
proof given, to justify the idea that that man's power was our work.
Have we forgotten that, from the time of the Constituent Assembly,
he already enjoyed an immense popularity, and that he obtained the
55 title of the Incorruptible? Have we forgotten that, during the
Legislative Assembly, his popularity only increased with the help of
a very widely-known journal of which he was the editor and
through his frequent speeches to the Jacobins? Have we forgotten
that, in the National Convention, Robespierre before long was the
60 man who, fixing all regard upon his own person, gained so much
confidence that it rendered him prepondant, to such an extent that
when he came to the Committee of Public Safety, he was already the
most important man in France? If someone asked me how he had
succeeded in gaining so much ascendancy over public opinion, I
65 would answer that it was by displaying the most austere virtues, the
most absolute devotion and the purest principles.

Jean-Nicolas Billaud-Varenne, *Mémoire Inédit*, R. T.
Bienvenue, op cit, p 317

Questions

a   How did the Law of 22 Prairial enable the Committee of Public
Safety to act 'with the speed of lightning' against traitors
(line 10)?
b   What evidence is there that extract *b* was written by a detractor of
Robespierre?
c   Does extract *c* suggest that Robespierre's character, described in
extract *d*, was destroyed by some of his supporters?
* d   Why did the Reign of Terror come to an end with the Ninth of
Thermidor?

5   Post-Thermidorian politics

(a) The reaction (1)

The severest justice must be used against all our country's enemies. Robespierre also used to say constantly that terror must be made the order of the day, and while with the aid of these words he had patriots incarcerated and led to the scaffold, he protected the rascals who were serving him. Yes, the Convention must strike them down; it is against these robbers of the public that it must wage eternal war. I no longer recognize castes in the Republic; I see in it only good and bad citizens. What does it matter to me that a man was born noble, if his conduct is good? What difference does the rank of a plebeian make, if he is a rascal! If the one disturbs the social order, he must be incarcerated; if the other robs the Republic, the law's blade must strike him; we must look for the people's enemies in official positions, in the administration, wherever they are; for, I repeat, in France there are only republicans or anti-republicans, who are rogues.

> Jean-Lambert Tallien, *Speech in the Convention, 2 Fructidor, Year II* [19 August 1794], R. T. Bienvenue, op cit, p 305

(b) The reaction (2)

The National Convention, after 9 Thermidor, was best and most surely placed to represent greatly the people's interests. There was in its position enough ability and power for the moral and political regeneration of the universe. Neither privilege nor king nor nobility nor the influence of the Catholic clergy nor foreign clerical power existed any longer; the parlements had been overthrown, the intermediate aristocracy shamed, the armies of the kings of Europe had been beaten, and they remained without energy; we had for us ardent youth who were going to arms with the enthusiasm of liberty and especially of equality; we had only to close ranks among civilians and to have the will. Unfortunately, passions were exacerbated. The deputies, who had perished in our dissensions, left successors in opinion [who were] always ready to rush into every kind of action to avenge them.

> Marie-Antoine Baudot, *Notes historiques* (ed. Mme Edgar Quinet, 1893), ibid, pp 339–40

(c) An émigré pamphlet

They [the French nobility] were there [at Coblenz] where their duty called them: they fled from a land where Louis sentenced them to death, without benefit to the throne, where he forbade them to rally to come to its defence. What crusade has been so blameless, so rightful! They cannot believe themselves to be separated from the nobility of all other countries. the people can be divided by nations and be strangers one to another; but the Nobility are one; no difference of climate, language or customs can divide them; they exist on the same bases, by the same privileges, and when these bases are attacked in a country, they are equally menaced in another. This is not a war of trade, frontiers or prestige: it is a war declared against all the power of rule, royalty, religion, morals, the hierarchy of ranks, privileges and property; all Sovereigns, Noblemen and Proprietors have the same interest in stifling it.

40

> *Annales historiques de la Révolution française* (1924), p 67

(d) An English view

It is very certain that the emigrants in many cities act with the usual imprudence of Frenchmen. Frequenting gambling-houses, etc., *car il faut vivre*. Running into debt is natural enough, and money borrowed is to return four hundred (on getting back to France) for twenty-five. I made it a point of frequenting the *tables d'hôte* in the different towns I passed through, and it appears three principles actuated the emigrants – *l'honneur, l'ambition et la crainte*. Two-thirds emigrated from ambition, and the other third may be divided between honour and fear. All the emigrants acknowledge this.

45

50

> F. Daniel to Mr Burges [probably 1794], J. M. Thompson (ed.), *English Witnesses of the French Revolution* (1938), p 232

(e) The Constitution of the Year III (1795)

We must be governed by the best citizens; the best citizens are those who are most educated and most interested in the keeping of the law. Now, with very few exceptions, you will find such men only among those who possess some property, who are attached to the country that contains it, the laws that protect it, and the peace that maintains it; men who owe to that property and to the affluence it affords the education which has made them fit to discuss wisely and equitably, the advantages and the drawbacks of the laws that determine the fate of the country. . . . A country governed by landowners is in a condition of social order, whereas one governed by persons other than property-owners is in a state of nature.

55

60

> François Antoine Boissy d'Anglas, *Moniteur* (réimpression XXV, p 81) in Georges Lefebvre, *The Thermidorians* (trans. Robert Baldock, 1965), p 189

Questions

a What is the difference of attitude towards the Thermidorian reaction expressed in extracts *a* and *b*?

b What can be learnt from extracts *c* and *d* about the character of the French nobility?

c   Is there a similarity of political outlook in extracts *c* and *e*?

d   'When the Thermidorians killed Robespierre, they killed the Revolution' (Robert Bienvenue). Do you agree with this statement?